Oranges at Christmas in a Communist Country

True Story

Second Edition

Cristina G.

authorcristinag.blogspot.com

To my parents who survived the Second War World,
and raised ten children under one of the most austere
communist regimes from Eastern Europe

***

A colossal Thank You to Dane Newman who
proofread this second edition after buying the eBook
from Amazon.com

Acknowledgements

A big Thank You to those who took the trouble to let me know about a few inconsistencies in the text.

Martin, Martine, Simone, Monica, Laura your constant support is priceless. I can't thank you enough.

Valentina, thank you for the oranges, I enjoyed them very much.

A massive Thank You to the reviewers who ignored my poor English language (as I insisted) and stood by my side in this long learning process. I am getting better day by day.

Thank you to everyone who shares and appreciates my work.

Thank you all for your understanding and care. It's touching.

Dane Newman, thank you again for your feedback. It helped me a lot.

May the universe be always on your side.

.

Preface

This is a fragment of my communist childhood—true to fact—and I have spent more than a year to build the courage to publish it.

I didn't write it for sympathy, but because it's a great story and deserves some notability. I believe that many of us could write at least one book about their lives.

I could write a dozen.

***

As you may have noticed, this is a Second Edition. Besides the grammar and spelling errors, only a few things—brought to my attention by some amazing readers as inconsistencies—were changed. Nothing major, so if you read the first edition, ignore this one for now.

What is Communism?

How old were you when you've discovered that Santa Claus was not a real person?

I was nine.

I am sure you have heard many stories about Communism. Some terrible, others not that much. While I was living in Italy and in England, I met people born in various communist countries. They all have different stories to tell the world. Mine was a thousand miles away.

Every communist country has its own system. Some governments are stricter than others. Some Rulers give less and pretend more from their people. But I didn't know anything about this until a few years back. I always thought that Communism was the same in every country on Earth.

It seemed that Romania was alone in Europe. It didn't respond to USSR or any other Political Power. Gorbachev visited my country often but Ceausescu wasn't very fond of him. I don't know much on the subject, so I'll stop here.

What I know is that I am the tenth child of a family of eleven. It was God's decision for me to come into this world, more of an incident if you want. Most definitely not a desired or planned child. Like my siblings and almost all children of that epoch though. My mother was forty when she gave birth to me in the middle of November 1975. She didn't have any real employment, as we intend it, but wasn't a housewife either, my mother was a slave on her own land.

Now, if you lived in my communist country and were a farmer, you know what I mean, but if you didn't, the word *slave* will sound extreme and make you feel I am overemphasising, except I am not.

The Communism period in my country started in 1948 with the king—*Michael I*— forced to abdicate and ended in blood in December 1989.

Communism, on paper, is an outstanding theory, "A system of social organisation in which all property is owned by the community, each person contributes and receives according to their ability and needs." —says Wikipedia. A Utopia I would say, and how many of these Utopias do you know of in this world?

Let me tell you in my words what Communism represented for my family. Please forgive my ignorance in politics, it is not something I would invest my time in.

Before Communism, my parents' families own several hectares of land, among other properties. They were considered wealthy farmers. They worked their land, raised animals and everything they had belonged to them. Others had goods, many were much wealthier than others, and some were even more: the boyars. There was a clear separation of social classes, but from what my parents told me, these rich people, boyars, were very good human beings and gave work to the poor.

My mother as a child, before her parents became wealthy, used to work for one of these boyars. He was a kind person and was used to give many presents to children on their birthdays, for example. He would come with bags full of candies, fruits, and various other things offering them to the celebrated of the day. They were not required to do that, it was a personal choice.

Now, I am sure you think that he was horrible regardless of these gifts because he employed children to work on his properties and that was inhuman. I couldn't agree more. I am telling you, it's how I always thought and sustained; however, we forget one fundamental thing here, back then, seventy years ago, more and less, that was considered absolutely normal. There were no laws that stated it was illegal to hire children and make them work for several hours a day. Things have changed a lot since then, although you'll still find adults exploiting children and not only in my country. We all know that. It is not my place to speak about this though.

When the Communism was imposed in the country, farmers and boyars with no exceptions were forced to put all their land together to form a collective.

When I say forced, it means that soldiers came with guns and tanks and pointed them directly at innocent people. Whoever refused the *new commandments* were killed on sight or cast into prisons, where they were badly tortured and left to starve to death on the cement floors of their cells. Many people died, hundreds, instantly shot dead.

All boyars were taken from their houses and sent to sleep in the middle of the street. After a life of hard work, everything they earned was confiscated by the state.

The farmers, after being deprived of their land, would still be owners on paper, and work the land, except that it wasn't for themselves, but for the greater good, the country.

You won't read about these atrocities in history

books because Communism is still a utopia for many.

I wasn't born yet, and I considered myself lucky to have not witnessed any of that. But my parents were, and you won't believe it, but they never said a word about this until the Communism had dissipated.

Why? Fear. Stories of entire families massacred circulated among people. My parents would have never risked our lives. They accepted the new lifestyle and imposed themselves to forget the past.

Husband and wife didn't speak a word between them, parents and children were afraid one of another. "Shh, even the walls have ears," my dad used to say. I came to learn all these things from my parents and other elderly people I got to talk to after the Communism—there weren't many left.

After the deprivation of goods and land, luckily, following certain criteria most were allowed to keep a piece of land attached to their houses for surviving purposes. Farmers lived off of the production from that soil. As I was saying, my mother and us, all farmers really, infant or elderly, were slaves on our land.

From March to late November six days a week, sometimes seven, my mother would wake up at four or five in the morning to cook for the family, then she'd go to various locations to do her part for the greater good. Twelve to fifteen hours each day, no matter the weather, physical conditions, or personal issues. There were no excuses, except for when the earth was oversaturated with water, from too much rain, and no being, human or animal, could walk on it.

My brothers and sisters, myself included, would go to school, mostly in the mornings, then would come home, get changed out of our uniforms into farmers' attire and reach my mother in the fields. Sometimes we would go to a different field that needed to be finished at the same time with the one my mother was working on. It all depended on the state, necessity, and requirement. One of us had to remain home to feed the animals, take care of the house, and cook dinner for everybody.

1975 has been a particularly busy and difficult year for the farmers in the country, especially for those from my region. It rained a lot, and all the harvests have been delayed by weeks or months. Winter had come, and the fields were covered in snow. It didn't matter though, the beetroots and the corn had to be cropped and the land prepared for the next year production.

Every new scholastic year started with two, three or even more weeks of hand-work on the fields. It wasn't an option, it was compulsory. The schools were asked to help because the adults weren't able to do all the work by themselves. Each family had a determined amount of production to deliver or a precise number of hectares to work on during each year. About how much was decided by the people in charge based on several criteria, one was the number of people in a family, parents, and progenies. The more children you had, the more you were required to produce and deliver. That decision was taken on the day one was born.

So you see, the day I came into this world, my family got additional land to work on, and I wasn't able to help out yet. I lived with this burden for years, since I was just a toddler.

Everybody thinks babies cannot interpret what is going on around them, but I don't how I was able to understand even before my birth when I was just a foetus in my mother's womb. I felt my mother's pain and struggle. I cried with her every time she felt blue. And she wasn't a happy soul. I don't remember, of course, but why else would I have been so sensitive, sensible, and responsible from such an early age?

**

You know by now that this story took place in a remote communist country situated in the East of Europe. There weren't many hospitals or doctors in that period of time, but there were a lot of midwives. That was because children in the communist era were considered a gold mine for the country. All women were encouraged and praised to remain pregnant as often as possible.

From 1960 to 1970 the number of births doubled in my country. In 1966 abortion was declared illegal. All this because the Communist Party (PCR) decided that the Romanian population should be increased from 23 to 30 million inhabitants. Just like that.

Women who had more than nine children were rewarded with a sum of money and with various certificates which made them feel valued. 1967 was the year in which the nation's population increased by 100%.

The story of my name

My mother worked the land for all the time she'd carried me, up until the morning I decided I wanted out. The night before, she went to her team leader and asked if she could stay home the next day because something made my mother think my birth due has come. She was afraid I will be born on some fields very far away from the village and getting back on time could have been impossible. But the team leader firmly denied. "Don't be ridiculous, Maria, if that comes, we will find a camion to take you to the maternity house. We can't let anyone home under any circumstances."

It wasn't an excuse; my mother knew her body well. I was the tenth child, of course she felt me kicking and preparing to get out any minute.

The worst part was that her team leader was a woman and a friend.

Great feminism support and demonstration of humanity, right? That was Communism itself, some paid a higher price than others.

It was 3 o'clock on a Friday morning when my mother woke up in terrible pain and realised that I had indeed decided to leave the safety of her belly for a place I knew nothing about.

The whole family was asleep, nine, no wait, eight children and my father. Two of my older sisters were already married and left the family by then.

My mother didn't say a word to anyone, as quiet as possible washed her face with cold water, put a few clean clothes into a plastic bag as quick as possible, and walked towards the maternity clinic from our village. Luckily, she didn't have to go far, just for five hundred metres. But every woman who gave birth would testify that when your water had broken, you cannot make any step without risking to let your child fall on the ground.

My mother has told me that she'd walked extremely slow, more crawling really and was utterly exhausted when getting there.

I cannot even begin to imagine the pain she must have been through. But the day I asked her how did she cope with it all, pregnancy, pain, birth. My mother said she was used to it and it wasn't such a big deal. That's why she didn't even think to ask someone to accompany her to the maternity house. It was her duty as a mother, nobody else's.

"What about someone to support you or carry your bag, what about dad? I was born from you, but he put me there," I said in shock.

"What do you think he could have done? Help me? How? I was the one who had to push. The only person it was needed to give birth to you it was me, and I was there. Ready to do my duty. Besides, the children had school, and your father had to go to work. There was no way that any of them would have been excused from doing what was required of them. They had their things to do, I had mine. All worked out well, isn't it? You see, there is no need for a second person when a woman gives birth. A woman can do everything on her own."

I cried when I heard her saying those words, I cried

because she's been forced to work while caring me inside, and all my other siblings, until the last minute. I cried for her force and courage, and I felt so guilty for making her go through all that alone. I couldn't understand why I had come into this world when I wasn't desired, for what purpose?

My parents had no clue about the gender of their tenth child as they didn't know of the first nine or the last one. There was no such thing as the amniotic fluid test. Only in science fiction books. It would not have changed anything, my parents were very religious people and abortion was considered a crime, thus a sin.

I came into the world screaming and kicking, and my mother got to be the first to know I was her seventh girl. 'My man won't be happy, he wanted a boy. What can we do? God makes happen whatever is already the plan for us. He's got no choice than to accept this girl,' thought my mother in her head.

I was a big, loud, girl with blue eyes that everybody expected will change colour in time. They didn't. Two days after my birth, my mother was asked what name should be written on the certificate. That moment my mother realised that she had no name in mind. My siblings usually helped her with that task, but whole my family hoped I was a boy. Nobody thought I would turn up a girl. My mother said she'll think about it and let them know as soon as possible. She had worked her brains out for hours, without success. She ran out of girl names. Understandable.

Then something happened. The midwife in charge was ill that day, therefore a replacement had to be provided because women gave birth every day in my village. An external midwife was in that day, and she had a baby boy of the age of three, approximately. As

These meetings were long ahead planned, and you had a free day (or half a day) from work or school. You were not allowed to be ill or about to give birth to a child, you had to be there. No matter what.

To be honest, from what I remember people were actually happy to have a free day from work so, when they got there, everybody was incredibly exuberant. People had to shout various slogans like "Viva Ceausescu! Viva the Communism Party!" at regular intervals, often prompted by a person from Ceausescu's staff. Everything was filmed and shown on TV every day.

Ceausescu loved travelling and visiting. He thought the country was doing amazingly well. Several stories are going around about how people from his staff used to prepare the land where he was foreseen with extreme care. If he wanted to see how apple trees were doing, people were required to take apples from other trees and attach them with a thread to the trees the president was expecting to have a look at. He only saw the trees carefully prepared for his inspection.

The same delicate operation took place with the corn fields. If a regular plant of corn could have had mostly one ear of corn, sometimes two (different sizes), all the plants Ceausescu saw had at least three huge ears of corn. Once again, people worked for days to attach these ears to the plant and make it look real.

Every time we saw these meetings on televisions, we had no doubt that those apple trees were a miracle of God because of the number of perfect fruits they had on their branches. Same with the corn plants. As farmers, we were incredibly amazed and envious of their harvest.

Due to all these tricks, I am inclined to believe that

Ceausescu was somehow kept in the dark from the real situation in the country. But of course, it is only my opinion.

How can anyone think that people could be happy and cheery when they don't have electricity in the house, no oil to cook and no bread to eat?

Rationalised food in the Golden Epoch

In 1981 Romania had to request the International Monetary Fund a line of credit and adopted a policy to pay back its debts. If before Romanians were okay with Ceausescu's dictatorship, that year they all started to feel pressured, used and dispensable. The food began to be rationalised, the power cuts were happening every day, same as the hot running water and central heating, no imports just export. The country was in total austerity, and the president couldn't care less. He had everything he needed and much more.

My family was doing fairly well, much better than others. That because we all worked night and day, no matter what. We had the necessary food for surviving, but chocolates and fruits were a luxury. And when you know you can't have something you want it even more.

The piece of land we had was reserved to growing vegetables. We couldn't afford to plant any sort of tree or grapes. Our neighbours had apple, pear, plum, cherry trees, and several types of grapes and we wanted so badly to have some too, but my father was against it because fruits were not considered nourishment, but a caprice. We exchanged some corn for apples or pears, but that was about it. We terribly craved for cherries and grapes every Autumn.

The first time I saw a banana I was seven maybe. My mother cut it into thin slices and when I tasted one, I thought was very disgusting and refused to eat more.

As I said, there was no chocolate to be found in the two shops of my village. Sometimes my older siblings would bring us some imported from Russia, bought illegally from people in the streets. It was the worst thing I tried in my whole existence back then. It had the exact texture and taste of plasticine. I promise. I tried plasticine when I was in kindergarten, not sure why, but that's how I know what Russian chocolate tasted like. Nobody liked it, not even the birds we raised.

Ironically, twenty kilometres away from my village was a huge chocolate factory, and one of my neighbours worked there. He used to bring home large cubes of raw chocolate, and something else called *glucose*. A sort of raw sugar used in the making of chocolate. His children always vaunt themselves with that, and we were quite envious.

We had loads of milk, cream, and made cheese every day. Every Saturday, my mother baked the most amazing sweet cheese pies in the world. All my siblings were raised in fear of God, and we've been taught that giving is one way to demonstrate you had a good heart, so we always shared our goods with everybody, especially with these neighbours of ours. They were truly poor and in need. However, they never gave us a piece of chocolate or glucose in return. I used to cry and complain with my parents, and my father would always say, "Cristinuza, sweets are not good for your teeth, health nor mind. You have the best food anyone could ever dream, be grateful for that and leave them alone. You don't need their stuff."

"But I give them cheese, and bread, and pies because they are always hungry and their parents never cook. Why can't they share some of their things with us? Why are them this way, Papa?" I would ask with tears in my eyes.

"People are all different, child. Don't be upset. God will always take care of us." My father will reply with sadness.

And when somebody reminded me of God, I would just fall in adoration as I was a true believer.

Anyway, my uncle used to bring us chocolates from time to time, proper and amazing chocolate, but I wanted glucose. That was the only sweet I ever liked as a child.

***

My family didn't know what vegetarianism was back then. We had no idea that there were people in the world who wouldn't eat meat, eggs, or cheese. We survived on these aliments. We raised many chickens, geese, turkeys, bunnies, pigs, and our father took care of cows for a living, and with the vegetables we grew on the land, we had absolutely everything you can think of. But all these animals, land and the slavery required loads of hard work. That's why every each of us did their part for the well-being of the family. Which meant we never had any spare time to play with other children. In fact, I have only random memories about this kind of activity.

But no matter how much food we had in the winter, there were some types of food we didn't have in the summer time. That because the meat or sausages were delicate and not having a fridge was quite a limitation. During the winter my mother used to cook all the meat in fat pigs and conserve it in huge jars. However, in the late summer, most of it was finished.

Therefore, we were constrained to go in the city to look for products from meat, especially when there was a big celebration close, like a village feast.

As I said, the food was rationalised, and there wasn't much to buy from the shops in my village anyway. Only some of the vital aliments like oil, bread, sugar, rice, and some sweets like biscuits and candies. A day a week in the summer time, one sold ice cream.

Families were given a ration book, and farmers were required to give to the state a percentage of all their goods. For example, if they had ten chickens, one had to be delivered to the shop when they went to buy the rationed food for the month. If they had hens, twenty eggs belonged to the state and so on. This was supposed to happen every four months. Not sure what kind of calculations were made and based on what. What I do know is that this didn't happen in the cities, but only in the rural areas. How did they know that you had or not? Well, at the beginning of each year, a census of people and everything they owned took place. You could have tried to lie or hide your birds or pigs, but random inspections were made and it they found something you omitted to mention, much more, or everything you had would have been taken away from you. It didn't matter you'd said that three of your chickens died or were stolen, or that you had to feed your children.

***

I remember once when my mother didn't have the last egg to take to the shop and the vendor refused to give her the rationed food for that month. My mother cried, begged, and promised she will bring the egg the next month because the hens made none in the last month. The vendor not only remained unwavering but insulted her in countless ways. She came home humiliated, crying her heart out. She was utterly desperate because she had no oil to cook dinner that evening.

I kneeled at her feet, held her hand and tried to calm her down but I couldn't. We both cried until no tears were left inside us. It was then I swore that I will do everything in my power and never allow anyone to mock my mother again.

The next day, my mother went to one of her sisters and begged for an egg, then went back to the shop and brought home the 100 millilitres per capita of sunflower oil, the rice, and the sugar. I wished we didn't have to eat so my mother wouldn't have had to bow her head in front of heartless humans.

I sometimes thought that it was better to have nothing because your ration would still have been given to you regardless. The more you had, the more you were required to give. By logic, if you had more, was because you worked more. But that didn't count.

Allow me to remind you (and me too) what the theory of Communism is, "a system of social organisation in which all property is owned by the community, each person contributes and receives according to their ability and needs." - Wikipedia

All my family, from children to elderly, worked for twenty hours a day to ensure we all had food on the table in each day of our lives. Some people had no idea of what work was, individuals who drank and slept the whole day but had same quantities of rationed food anyway.

In the cities, people had jobs and paid taxes, but that was about it. My mother worked on her land for the country, received no money in return, and was forced to share her chickens with the state. Moreover, in villages, you couldn't find milk, eggs, any product made from meat, chocolate, toys, or fruits. Left aside the fact you couldn't find clothes, shoes, shampoo, or soap.

When the harvest of grain was good, we baked bread once or twice a week, but there were years in which the state kept everything for itself, so we were forced to buy bread. I wasn't so fond of bread, I preferred polenta a thousand times more; however, cold polenta in the winter time wasn't that delicious. At home, we were able to make fresh polenta at any time, but my father needed to have lunch at work—he left the house every morning at 4 or 5 AM and came back at 7 PM—therefore, a piece of bread was a must.

They didn't sell bread every day in our village shop. I don't know if it was because farmers were supposed to have grain or corn and bake their own bread, or because nobody gave a damn on us. Usually, when the rumours reached my family that on a certain day bread was expected to be sold in the village, my mother used to send me to stay in line and buy at least two loaves (of 270 or 320 grammes each). Because we were eight siblings and two parents, two loaves were a joke, but it was better than nothing. We treated it as a delicacy.

Nobody knew the exact time of the day the bread will get there, so people would wait for hours in an Indian queue in front of the shop. However, when the vendor would open the doors to let us in, all that order became a total chaos in a matter of seconds. Every time. I was just a child, 5-11 years old, but the others were strong adolescent males. I was often pushed aside or thrown on the ground and stepped on with no mercy. Most of the time, even if I was the first one in the queue, in one second I would become the last, and I would cry, beg and shout in despair. A fight for life and death because I knew there weren't enough loaves for everyone. The thought of going home empty handed terrified me. That would have resulted in no lunch for my father for the next day. I couldn't stand that. I didn't want my father to suffer hunger when he worked for so many hours a day. It was the least I could do for him.

One day they started to sell two loaves per person in the queue, and I was euphoric. Usually, they only sold one. My heart was racing from a mix of excitement and fear. I was afraid that the bread will end before I got the chance to buy any. I was praying all Gods in the universe, as every time I was in a queue; however, when it got my turn, the vendor decided to sell me only one piece. With tears on my cheeks, I complained right away asking for two, as the person in front of me, "I have got seven siblings at home, plus my parents. It is not fair."

Do you know what the vendor did? He refused to sell me any because I was too *arrogant*.

Luckily, people were on my side and joined me in the protest, "Give her two loaves, she's a part of the most numerous family in the village. One will never be enough. Don't you have a soul?" The vendor knew me very well because I was often seen with my mother, but he couldn't care less. To be honest, I am sure he didn't like any of my family members and did that on purpose. However, when everybody started to shout at him, he had no choice than giving me two and let me go. I went outside with the dress tore apart and full of bruises, but with happiness inside my soul. "I did it! I did it!" I shouted with pride, hugged the loaves, and ran home as fast as I could. That was a lucky day for me, and we didn't have many during that period.

That happened in the village, but in the cities, they

sold more than two loaves, and you didn't need a ration book for it. Back then, because bread was made from wholemeal, most people thought they were only good to feed the pigs. Personally, I preferred it to the white bread, like all my other siblings. My father was never bothered of what he ate unless it was cold polenta which he never liked. My mother's favourite was the white bread, but she was alone in that.

Going to the city required to buy a bus ticket, more money to spend and not all people in the village were willing to do that. We needed bread in order to survive, especially when there was a scarcity of flour in our reserves, my mother would ask me if I wanted to go and buy at least ten or fifteen loaves at one time. And with that occasion, I always went and brought to my sister some potatoes and random vegetables of the period. I was just a child and ten kilogrammes of potatoes were extremely heavy, but I never said no. Not even because I was utterly terrified to travel by bus. If I had to be at school by 8 AM, I would wake up at 4 AM and take the first bus into the city. From there I would first go and leave the heavy bags at my sister's place. I needed at least thirty minutes to get there, and from there I would run like the best athlete in the world, get into the first shop, buy as many loaves they would sell me, then search for another one, and buy others until I had no more space in my two huge bags. Luckily, fifteen loaves of bread were not as heavy as ten kilogrammes of potatoes.

The last step was the shop in the bus station. In there they always sold me as many loaves I wanted, if I had the money. I could have run from my sister's place to there without a stop, but I was never sure I would find any bread in there. Sometimes there was none left, and it happened to me once. I had to go back into the city to look for bread in other shops and missed the bus to the village. After that, I could have never taken the chance to buy all the necessary bread from there. But I always checked, even if my bags were full. On that period, the plastic bags were rare as gold. My uncle left some to us, and I used to carry one with me all the time, just in case. When the shop from the bus stop had bread, I'd spent all the money I had left on my last bread of the day. My mother was always so happy when I got home with fifteen or twenty loaves. That meant we could all have as much bread as we felt like for almost a week. We didn't have butter or margarine, those were delicacies, and we only bought some to make cakes or cookies for special days. However, we had quince or apple jam to spread on top of it. Not only that, my father exchanged milk with a sort of dark wine marmalade which we loved immensely. What a treat for all of us.

Meat, sausages, bacon, generally meat products were not that easy to find in the city close to us. For that, we needed to get up at 2:30 – 3:00 AM, walk for six kilometres on foot and travel for at least seventy by train. I was a very strong, resourceful, and resilient child but that trip was too dangerous to be made alone; therefore, my mother would always send me when at least two other adults would express their desire to go to that city with the same reason as mine. Many times I came home with nothing in my bag, completely exhausted and disappointed. My mother never got upset. It wasn't my fault in the end, she knew that I always did my best in everything. If my bag was empty, it meant that there was no meat at all anywhere.

What's been bothering me for all these years is how

come that period was called *The Golden Epoch*? Who gave it this name? Based on what? The dictator's style of life?

School, pioneers, and books

Going to school was compulsory in my country, thank God for that! All Ceausescu's speeches contained the following slogan borrowed from Lenin, "Study, Study, and Study again."

However, this maxim wasn't addressed to farmers' children. The country survived on agriculture. Farmers were not really required to go to school, just on the land. But nobody ever made this distinction in public. The Communism's theory was that we all had the same rights.

For many children going to school was a burden, for me was the best thing in the whole world and I loved it with all my heart. From a very early age instead of playing, I sat in the corner of the bed and watched my older sisters writing or reading. I could not understand how anyone can create a word from nothing, then phrases from words, furthermore, entire stories from phrases. It seemed a sorcery back then, and I was absolutely fascinated. I envied them so badly, and I couldn't wait to be able to do it myself.

It is common practice for children to be taught writing and reading as soon as possible. Some are starting at the age of two, and by the time they reached five they already know how to put words onto paper. Not me, and not my little brother. I don't know about my older siblings. I guess it was tradition in my country not to do the educators' job. They didn't teach that in the kindergarten, we had to be six to go to school and learn the secret of knowledge. But I couldn't wait any longer, and in July of 1981, I started asking my mother to send me to school.

After my little brother's birth, my mother was diagnosed with a heart disease. As a result, she wasn't able to go to work the land every single day as always. So when she was home, in the morning before going to kindergarten, then in the afternoon, in the evening, and before going to be, I would say these words over and over again, "Mum, please, send me to school. I want to be able to read as my older siblings." She would look funny at me and laugh at first, but when I started to beg and shed countless tears, my mother took me seriously and went to speak with the school director. Unfortunately, there were rules, you must have turned six before the 14th of September, the new scholastic year, to be accepted in school. I was born in the middle of November, so I was five years and ten months old. Too young.

I was devastated by the news, and I cried, kicked and pulled my hair out. I ran away in the garden, rolled my body into a ball and sobbed for hours until my father came home and tried to take me inside by force. I didn't want to give up, and I kept insisting. Then I stopped eating, and my parents worried. I heard them discussing the situation, and many harsh words were spoken. My mother said she already tried, my father demanded her to try again and she started crying, "Why don't you go to speak with him? You are her father; your name is respected, and your words have more weight. You always let me deal with the education of our children, it is not fair. I cannot do everything on my own."

"I cannot miss a day of work; we need the money to buy things for the other four children who are about to start a new scholastic year in a while."

My mother was crying, and my little brother didn't understand what was going on, so he started sobbing too. I felt so guilty for have been the cause of those countless fights between my parents. It was heartbreaking witnessing to such a habitual scene. I sat in the corner of the living room and joined them in the weeping. My father couldn't stand the sight of such emotions and demanded us to stop. It was easier said than done. We went to bed with our eyes inundated by tears, like many other nights before.

A week after, I asked again, and my mother had a brilliant idea. She brought my little brother into consideration, "Who'll take Sebastian to kindergarten? He's still too young to go and stay alone in there. Plus, the best teacher in the village will start a new generation of students next year. It's in your best interest to wait another year."

I cried again, but my mother had put on the table very valid arguments. Besides, there was nothing anyone can do. Too many children in the village. Each generation had four classes of thirty-two students, there wasn't a single free place. I had to accept it and move on. I wanted so badly to be able to read and write, but nobody even considered to teach me the alphabet's letters at home. Or maybe they did consider it, but nobody ever mentioned it though. Everybody was busy with their studies, the chores around the house, and on the land.

At the end of August, my mother went into town to buy uniforms for my older siblings, two boys, and two girls. Four of my other siblings, all girls, were already moved out my parents' house. Three of them were married, the other one was going to a boarding school.

I was envious and heartbroken, but there was nothing anyone could do.

***

I went to school in 1982, when the country was in total despair.

In August that year, my mother went to stay in an endless queue to buy me all the necessary for school, pencils, erasers, crayons, block notes, drawing blocks, various books. I was so excited and kept running on the street to see my mother coming with the bags full of those wonders of which I have dreamed for years. She came home five hours later, completely exhausted. That shop was just twenty minutes away. It was normal, so nobody complained.

When my mother gave me the heavy bag, I started crying from emotion. I couldn't believe that I was soon to become a student. I opened it and looked through everything. I touched every object, smelled it, and thought I was the luckiest child in the whole universe. What I liked most was the black fountain pen. Back then, it was compulsory to write with the fountain pens. Regular pens were prohibited. I really don't know why. My mother asked me to be careful with it not only because was expensive, but mostly because they couldn't be found anywhere until the following year.

Then my mother went to the city and bought my first uniform. A dress with small blue and white squares, plus a blue sort of apron, both made from cotton.

I was so in love that everybody thought I was

completely out of my mind. No child was happier and eager to go to school than me. My family took me for a freak, but I didn't care.

I loved the first day of school, even if I was all shaky and terrified. The school had three distinct buildings in its precincts. The oldest one was reserved for the primary school, the newest for the secondary, and another in between for the college and library. The rooms had no central heating, and the school had no science laboratories or computers.

The bathroom was a separate building with no running water. But I was happy, and I didn't know children around the world had better conditions. I was living a dream and I have always been all eyes and ears during the classes. I wouldn't have missed a minute of it, ever, under no circumstances. I promised that I will go to school dead or alive. Best period of my life.

The letters were a miracle. We learned a new one every day, and in less than a month I was able to read and write without any help. I thought I would die from happiness. My first dream came true! Because my voice was clear and powerful, the teacher, Maria, used to ask me to read for the class every day. I didn't like that at all, but I always listened and did what was asked of me.

Then I went to the library and borrowed my first book, *Les miserable*, by Victor Hugo. The librarian thought I was too young for such a book, but I insisted and promised I will give up reading it if I couldn't understand what was all about in the first ten pages. Do you think I could let that book off my hands until I finished it? Yes, I left it because I still went to help my siblings and my mother on the land, I still helped with the chores in and around the house. I kept feeding the pigs, the birds and continued cooking. But when the night came, and the lights were switched off, that's a metaphor because the lights were already off from the dictator's decision, I would go into my room, light a candle and moved into a different world. I cried so much and felt the pain of those poor children. I wished I could help them... but who was helping me?

When I took the book back, three days later, the librarian was quite impressed. At least it's what I thought until a few months later when she proved me wrong. After that first book, I asked if I could have two books at once. I didn't have much time to go to the library. She wasn't very happy, but gave them to me, but not after I promised I would actually read them and not go through the pictures only. I didn't understand what she meant with that.

I took the books back in three days again, she looked at me with scepticism, but still gave me the other two books I asked for. My new favourite author was another illustrious French name, Jules Verne. I devoured his books with incredible fervour. The worlds he transported me in were absolutely magical. They were incredibly easy and fast to read. The next time I dared to ask for three books at once. The librarian refused categorically. I begged and promised I will take them back on time. When she denied my request again, I brought to the table that she just lent three books to another student. "I saw it with my eyes minutes ago. You cannot be so unfair towards me," I cried.

"Child, that student is in the secondary, you're in the primary! Do you see why I am so reluctant to lend you so many books at once?" explained the librarian.

"I promised I can handle them. They are easy books, and I am a very fast reader. Please! I won't leave this room without these three books."

She had no choice but giving them to me. "But you don't have to bring them back in three days, take your time. You have two weeks. Okay?" shouted the librarian after I grabbed the books and ran outside the darkroom.

I was holding those books as they were the most precious thing I ever had in my hands, and I was immensely happy. I thought I could do anything when I was reading.

When I took them back, five days later, the librarian made me sit and interrogated me about the content of all of them. Only then I realised that the look in her eyes wasn't positive. I answered all her questions, and she was still not convinced.

"It's hard for me to believe that a child could read so many books in five days. Do you do your homework? What are your parents saying when they see you bringing home all these books?" asked the librarian.

"I just love reading, I do my homework every day. I don't miss a day of school because I love studying. As for my parents, they don't know I read, they think I study. They are very severe and strict about learning and being good in school. I am a good student, you can ask my teacher, Maria, if you don't believe me. She'll tell you everything about me." I omitted to mention that I was also helping with the chores in and around the house, with the land, and my mother with the weaving. She would have definitely thought that I was lying or maybe she would have accused my parents of exploiting me. Which wasn't true at all. I was the one offering all the time.

I was indeed a good student, and my teacher was very fond of me. I always had fantastic grades, and I was among the elite in the class. However, at the end of the year, when I was expecting a first or second prize, along with my parents, at the very last minute, it was given to somebody else. A student, two or three students who weren't supposed to have any prize whatsoever. I never cared, but my parents felt very humiliated and discriminated. We all knew why. Corruption and blackmail were very popular in my country. During those times if a powerful parent went to a teacher and asked them to give their child a prize, although they didn't deserve it, the teacher had to agree. For a reason or another. Maybe an amount of money was put on the table, maybe offers of favours or even menaces.

One year, I don't remember if it was the first or the second, or even the third grade, the teacher came to me and asked for forgiveness because she had no prize for me although I deserved it. She was in such distress. I am not sure how I reacted because I don't have any memories after her confession. Maybe I was too upset and imposed my mind to forget, as I did with many other bad experiences in my life, just to be able to move on and forgive. But I don't think I was too upset, just very disappointed.

She's long gone now, may she rest in peace, and I don't have anything against her. I genuinely loved her despite the fact she gave my prizes away. She always showed me that she cared and was good enough for me.

We all went to school, my parents were very strict about it, especially my father. Under no circumstances, any of us would stay home from school. Ever. Unless you were, of course, very ill. But we were all quite healthy children mostly because the food we ate was free of chemicals and we also spent loads of time outside, under the sunshine, running wild and filling our lungs with fresh air. Our brain was very well oxygenated at any time of the year, as you can imagine. All my siblings were born with quite a quantity of intelligence. They were fast thinkers and learners, therefore set as examples to follow. The only thing that we were missing was confidence, so it was very rare that we would raise our hands to give a correct answer when educators and teachers asked the class. Luckily, some of them were very good at understanding human behaviour and would call our names to provide the answer when nobody else has come up with one. We've never failed to impress them, but it wasn't enough to exceed in a world of discrimination and censures.

I loved helping my family with everything I could, but I also loved school. It was a parallel universe, and I never missed a day. Maths, grammar, literature, and languages were my favourite classes. Nowadays, children around the world learn to read and write at a very young age, three, four, five or even earlier. I learned all these at seven. My parents tacitly empowered my older siblings with the education of the youngest generations but didn't have time to teach me.

***

Everybody was a communist when my mother gave birth to me, but you weren't born into it. Nevertheless, there was no choice; nobody asked you if you wanted to be one or not.

I remember the day I became part of Romania's pioneer movement (future communists) with all my colleagues. I was at the elementary, eight years of age. The date was prefixed by the school, and we were all very emotional. I had no idea of what I was doing back then, it was required and considered an honour, that's what we've been told. We had an asseveration ceremony, and red cravats with our country flag on the borders of it were given to us. They even rewarded us with a school day trip, paid by our parents, though, which weren't very happy about it. We went to visit the Neamt Citadel, a medieval fortress built in the 14th century. Restored in 2007, it looks quite impressive now but back then they were just some ruins, and I could not understand why we were there, to see what exactly? To be honest, there is a rich and important history about it, but my interest in history wasn't very deep.

The trip was a tradition, every new generation of pioneers visited the same place.

I thought my father was a communist, my mother too, but it wasn't quite the same for them as they weren't students when the king was forced to abdicate in the favour of Populism or Communism. They were still children, but because of the Second World War, they had no school to go to; therefore, they weren't proudly invested as pioneers. My father wasn't an actual farmer as he had a day job in the city. In there he was approached and tempted by an offer of money to become a Communist Party member, but he didn't accept it. Refusing to become an active communist was considered treason, and you could have lost your freedom and your life in one instant.

My father was a man with strong principles and couldn't betray them. As he was a very hard and reliable worker, plus a respected father, his rare case was not brought to the attention of the men in power; hence he never had a communist ID.

My mother was never asked or offered to become a member of the Communism Party as she was just a farmer. Her participation would have never counted for anything. Farmers were not deserving, farmers were slaves.

I didn't even know there was anyone in the country not being a communist. I never questioned this, and my parents never spoke about it; it was just an assumption I made.

Children were required to help the adults at the collective (all the land took from the owners and put together). Every new scholastic year started with a period of hard work for all students, no matter the age. It wasn't an option; you had to go and gather onions, potatoes, tomatoes, corn and so on. Whatever needed to be done first.

The parents sent the children to school, and the school sent the students on the fields. My father would always get upset when hearing such barbarity. This happened in villages and maybe only in my region. I really don't know. What I do know is that my assistance was required to help reach the targets. It was a rule of the Communist government, one of many. Gifted with a deep sense of duty I've never complained when coming back from school I was expected to take care of the house, feed the animals and work on the land for the family or the state. It didn't seem unfair or outrageous to me, on the contrary, I felt I was doing my duty. To be honest, I always offered, since I can remember. It was the least I could do. Someone had to do it. If my other siblings were busy with studying, I would just step in and do whatever needed to be done to the best of my ability.

One day, when I was six, they were debating who was going to stay home and cook dinner. I have a sister who wasn't very fond of cooking, so she would always try her best to persuade someone else to do it for her.

That day I said I'll do it. They all looked at me in disbelief. I was a little too young to cook for eight people (two of my older sisters were already married and had their children at that time). I was asked if I had ever cooked before.

"No, but I can do it. I watched mum doing it. It's no big deal," I said convinced.

"All right then, it is settled. Give it a go," they said unwillingly. There was a lot to be done in the fields that day, in all honesty, they had no choice as I was really too small to deal with the quantity of the production expected to be delivered that day.

I gave it a go, so to speak. I didn't do an exceptional job but trust me when I tell you that I was very happy for have been trusted with the cooking as I was very passionate about it. I cooked potatoes with meat and a huge polenta. I wasn't tall enough to reach the stove and stir the food, so I put a wooden box under my feet. It worked perfectly. The dinner was ready when my siblings came home from the fields, and they were all quite impressed. Same as my father and my mother who came home much later than all. We might all have been asleep by that time. I don't even remember seeing her every day.

My father looked at me in wonder and told me to be careful not to set the house on fire next time. The stove worked with wood, but we didn't have much during the Communism as we preserved our trees and forests, therefore we used corn cobs or the whole plant dried. It was a cheap and fast way to cook, but also dirty and very dangerous. It required constant attention. So, yes, it was demanding, but I never ran away from tough tasks.

My mother's art

There were four seasons in my country, all very clearly delimited by the weather. During each of them, the land had to go through various stages of production.

I start with the winter, my favourite season. It used to snow a lot, and the temperatures would always drop around minus thirty Celsius degrees. You might think that during this period farmers would rest and charge their batteries for the next year of hard work, and you are right. Most farmers were doing just that, except a few families like mine. We didn't go to play in the snow making snowmen as our mother never stopped working every single day of the year, except Sundays—God's day. She was a handloom weaver. There were a few women in the village doing the same, but she was a true artist, The Best. You might think I am biased, but you'd change your mind if you saw my mother's work. Hundreds of rugs weaved by her hands were sold in the markets, thousands of metres of different styles of tapestries are to be found in several houses in my village and not only. She earned a degree of fame in that period. People would come from far away to buy a rug made by my mother as her work would stand out from thousands. Her artwork was easy on the eyes and filled people's heart with joy. Every piece was impeccable, each colour was perfectly balanced, and no mistake was ever to be found in any of them.

She was a perfectionist and would have never finished a piece knowing it was a mistake in it. If the fault wasn't captured until the very end, she would unweave every centimetre to get there and fixed it. Unweaving takes a considerable amount of energy and quadruples the time. The flaw might have been invisible to everybody's eyes, but not hers. She would spot one from several metres away.

My mother never rested during the winter when the land was frozen, so we couldn't either because she needed the thread and wool prepared, ready to be used for the rugs. Wool was easy to find and set up but had terrible faults. First, moths loved it; secondly, the colour would wash off very easily, therefore my mother would only work with synthetic wool. This had brighter and forever stable colours plus an impressive durability. A piece, which would take my mother four or five months of daily work, was going to remain intact and eternal.

We, children, after doing the homework, were assigned to prepare the thread, forming perfect clews of wool. The five months of winter would go by like that every year. Personally, I loved every single day of it.

The snow covered everything with thick layers, sometimes three or four metres of fluffy and cold white material. The view was breathtaking. Pure magic. Never seen anything more idyllic than that in my life.

We went to school walking on the snow, then coming home, completely frozen got changed and sit around the terracotta stove listening to the crackling fire and my mother's weaving. The whole family united was heaven on earth for me. Priceless memories.

***

When the snow started to melt, spring would hesitantly settle in. Every snowdrop's birth indicated the time has come for the land to be ploughed and sown.

Most farmers were anxious to go out after a long period of lethargy. As we never rested, we were already tired.

***

When summer showed up, the young plants needed weeding. This process was very demanding and required certain skills, caring and patience as it had to be done at least two times consecutively. You would finish weeding all the land you had once, then you had to start all over again because the weed would grow faster than the plants. You couldn't afford to omit the second weeding as the production would tremendously drop, at the point that you wouldn't have a harvest period because there was nothing fully matured.

This was valid only for the piece of land exploited for your family survival. The state wouldn't control what you've done on your crop, it was your own business.

My family, for example, divided the soil situated behind the house, in many small crops. Every single metre was destined for growing a specific vegetable, herb, corn, or potato.

We had no flowers and no fruit trees, we couldn't afford any waste of fertile soil. Trees were growing big, and their branches would have prevented the sunlight to caress the crops. We had no idea that there were fruit trees that don't grow big back then.

We loved fruits a lot, especially cherries and grapes, but fruits were not considered food (as I said before), and although we've asked and cried to have at least an apple tree planted, my father decision was final. If there was something I really missed, was a tree fruit. I had many dreams about this for years.

Flowers were out of the question, no discussion allowed. Ever.

***

September was the start of Autumn. The Schools would open for a new year of studying and all the work done during the whole year on the land would finally show their fruits. Every single farmer, from an early age, was required to help with the harvest. Many parents were very protective of their children and never expected them to do such a demanding job, but the government had a different opinion, "Children need to be taught to do everything and take care of themselves as soon as they got rid of the diapers. It's for their own good."

I must admit that I agree to that now, as I agreed back then, still, most of the time we were forced to work for several hours without fresh water or a break. Many were crying from fatigue and dehydration, but the schools had to give their contribution for the greater good. Students had to help finish the harvest. No matter what, no excuse. But only the students from villages were submitted to this sort of treatment. As I said, people living in the cities had no land to give to the state and work on. They had jobs in the factories, and that was their contribution. Except they were paid to do it, were entitled to holidays and free days, and when the time has come for them to retire, they would have a good pension to live from.

From my experience, farmers were deprived of their properties and forced into slavery. They weren't paid in money but were given a percentage of the whole year production. If the year was poor, you didn't receive anything. Farmers were given the permission to retire at least five years later than the factory people, and their pension was a joke. No person was able to survive on that money.

Please forgive me for reminding you again what Communism is, "each person contributes and receives according to their abilities and needs."

Autumn Harvest

I've never liked Autumn. For a farmer, it is the most demanding season. Both physically and psychologically. The weather was bad, it rained a lot, and the unpaved roads of all villages were full of mud and puddles. The days were shorter, and the sun stopped to shine. It was cold, windy, and dark. People were always in the fields, completely drained of energy.

Women were also in charge of making jams and various canned vegetable stews for the winter. The legume and vegetable production had to be conserved for the long winter to come. We had no fridge if you remember.

Farmers were working incessantly with little sleep. Children were going to school from where they were taken into the fields to help the *Collective* with the last step in the agriculture system. Nothing could have been postponed no more. It didn't matter it was raining or even snowing, the harvest had to be finished at any cost. There was a lot of pressure from many sides.

I couldn't stand the dirt. I loved the green of the fields and the trees. The dead leaves on the ground were the clear sign that nature was slowly dying. The landscape had a very daunting look. All things were either brown or grey. I felt cold every day, deep down in my bones. Every morning I would go outside, had a look around and started to shiver uncontrollably.

Everything and everyone looked utterly miserable.

A Saturday morning, my father woke me up to go and harvest the beetroots. My mother was ill, my siblings were in charge with our crop from behind the house, so my father took a few days off to help us finishing the work on the land before winter. I was eight maybe, and I didn't have school on weekends. It was still completely dark outside and inside, that's why my father was holding a candle in his hands. I had a quick look at the clock which indicated it was 5: 30 AM. "Papa, I am so cold and tired today," I murmured.

"I know, child, I know. But we had to collect the beetroots and send them to the Sugar Factory to be processed. We cannot postpone this any longer. Your mother doesn't feel very well today; we are the only ones who can do this. Hurry up, I'll wait outside," said my father while placing the candle in a glass full or corn flour. "Don't forget to blow on it before you leave, so it won't burn without a purpose."

"Yes, Papa. Don't worry, you know you can trust me."

I looked at my siblings sleeping in various beds in the room, they seemed so peaceful. I moved as slowly as possible, dressed up, blew on the candle and left the room five minutes later.

Outside, I washed my face with fresh cold water from a bucket. We didn't have running water in the house, what we had instead was a fountain, twenty metres deep. We used buckets to take the water out. I am sure you don't have any idea of what I am talking about, as you might have never seen something like that in your life. Anyway, it was quite dangerous for a child to use this fountain. It required strength and a certain height.

My father started coughing, it was a false cough to make me aware of the fact he was waiting.

"I need to go to the toilet, Papa. I am not a robot."

"Hurry up," he said, "we need to be ready when the cart arrives, there is a lot to do."

"I know that, but I have needs as all beings. You can start walking without me, I'll reach you in about two minutes."

It was cold and windy as every day of the last week. I looked at the sky emptied of stars, 'It's cloudy. I hope it won't rain. God, please, don't let the rain fall today. We need to finish the beetroot harvest.'
My father is way ahead of me, and I started running and reached him one minute later.

"Stop running," he said, "you don't want to hurt yourself. Who'll work the land and help your mother with the house and the weaving?"

"I won't hurt myself," I said and asked myself, 'Is it really only this the reason that my father doesn't want to see me hurt? I refuse to believe that!'

My father was carrying a few things, so I tried to take the sickle and the bag with food and water from his hands. "I will carry them; I am stronger than you. Save your energy for the harvest, you'll need them."

We walked in silence for at least fifty minutes. There was no living soul on the unpaved streets, no animals, no humans. The village was still asleep. I was thinking of the homework I needed to do that weekend, Sunday or maybe that night before going to bed if it wasn't going to be too late.
We finally reached our piece of land. The dawn was settled, and we were able to start working.

"I am hungry, Papa, can I eat something?"

"Why didn't you eat before leaving the house?

There is no time!" he snapped out.

"But Papa...." I thought of trying to reason with him, but I knew it was pointless. 'I'll survive,' I said to myself.

Suddenly my father took out a piece of bread from the bag and handed it to me in silence. I grabbed it with tears in my eyes and started chewing on it, holding the bread in one hand and the sickle on the other one. I raised my head and had a long look at the piece of land full of beetroot.

"How long do you think it will take us, Papa? Do you think we'll finish by three in the afternoon like we did last year?"

"That's impossible. You are just a child."

"But last year were just us two again, and it was all done by two in the afternoon, Papa. Why are you always so pessimistic? It's not good, Papa, I have told you so many times."

My father looked at me betraying mix feelings, anger, and wonder. But said nothing, spit on his hands and grabbed the first beetroot by the brown leaves. One second later the beetroot came out of the ground full of brown soil. My father cleaned it up with one hand and used the sickle to cut the leaves off. He then threw it on the earth, three metres ahead of him. It's where we made the first heap of beetroots.

I took another bite of bread and started doing the same. Some beetroots were easy to dig up, others not so much. Twenty minutes later, the first heap was behind us, and we started the second one. Father worked one metre away from me. We didn't speak, just focused on the job. I was all sweaty and breathing heavily. 'Les Miserables we are,' I thought, but didn't say anything.

The sun was out now, and I didn't even notice it for a while. It was hot, and I was thirsty. I looked for the bottle of water, but the bag was quite far away.

"Papa," I shouted, "I am going to bring the water, do you want some?"

He didn't answer so I started running toward the end of the croft. I found the bottle and drank as much as I could. It was already tepid, but I didn't mind. I grabbed all the things and went back fast, giving the bottle to my father. He took it and drank the half of it. He was thirsty too, maybe even dehydrated, but he didn't want to waste time going back to take the bottle from the bag.

"It's warm. Soon we'll have to go and bring some fresh one," he said. Then looked at me and asked how everything was going.

"It's going well. I am positive will finish by the time Uncle John reaches us."

"The harvest is low this year; the beetroots are quite small," my father replied.

"I don't think so, Papa. Last year was much worse, don't always complain. God will punish us by taking it all from us. You know how it works."

His brown eyes were very sad, and my heart was bleeding for him.

"We'll be fine, Papa, don't worry. God will help us, have faith."

"What kind of child are you? How do you know these things? Who's teaching you religion?"

"I read loads of books," I replied. " And when I go to church, I listen carefully."

"You read? When?! You should do your homework, not read! The school is important."

"Reading is learning. I read when I can, in my school breaks..." - 'during the night,' I thought, but I didn't say it out loud as he would have gone ballistic on me.

"You sure are something, child... let's go back to work."

"When will we have lunch? I am hungry again."

"Midday," he looked at the sun and continued, "in about one hour."

"How do you know what time it is? You don't have a watch."

"It's the sun, look carefully. You'll learn to know the hour by looking at the sun as you've learned to read the clock. Remember?"

I didn't reply and went back two years in my memory when my father taught me the time reading. It seemed impossible at first and thought I was never going to learn. Every couple of minutes my father asked what time it was and a few hours later, I knew every each of them. How proud of myself I felt!

"You need to know the time, so you won't be late to school. We'll not always be here to wake you up," he used to say.

I had another long look at the crop trying to understand when we'll be finishing it. I bent again with the sickle in my hand and pulled out with force every single beetroot from my parcel.

"Be careful with that sickle, don't cut yourself, alright?" shouted my father.

I didn't reply as I was in a parallel universe where I was lying on a bench reading thousands of books. Someone called my name from a distance. I was daydreaming and didn't answer. I couldn't come out to reality. I wanted to sit on a bench and read.

"Cristinuza, it's midday, come to eat. Hello? Do you hear me?"

I raised my head and saw my father waving both hands. I had no choice but changing universes. "I am coming," I said while putting down the sickle and walking towards my father. He was holding the bag with food. "Do you know what your mother's prepared for us today?"

"No," I replied. "I hope we have boiled eggs. Mum cooks them to perfection. Not too soft and not too hard. Amazing. I think she's a witch."

I opened the bag and looked inside. I took the small rug from it and put it on the soil so we could sit on it. There was plenty of food, eggs, cheese, polenta, pork. I was very happy while preparing the picnic, as I used to call it.

"Papa, will you sit for a few minutes, please? You need to rest. Fifteen minutes, not more."

"There is no time, I'll stand."

I looked at him with sadness and he changed his mind. He sat and tried to take his black Wellington off, but it was impossible. "Do you want me to help you?" I asked.

"No, it's fine. I don't have to do that. I don't know what I was thinking, it's just midday, not the end of the day!"

"Your feet are on fire I guess. Those boots are like a stove when it's sunny... pity it doesn't feel the same way during the winter."

We were both eating absently. We looked around as other people were doing the same. It was either a tradition or an imitation of one another. I don't know, but it happened all the time. As soon as someone sat for lunch, others were following. Maybe a tacit understanding or a farmer's pact.

It was a very hot day of Autumn and felt like more like Spring. I loved Spring, it was my second favourite after Winter.

I took one boiled egg and opened it with a teaspoon. I was curious to know if my mother's done it again. I was always amazed by her ability to cook eggs to absolute perfection.

I love boiled eggs and tried many times to cook them the way my mother does, but they are always either too hard or very much uncooked. I asked her how she did it once, so she's explained it in detail, "I put cold water in the cauldron, add the eggs and as soon as the water starts boiling, I count to 120 and take them out."

"120?! Why this number?" I asked surprised. "It sounds like a sorcery to me."

"It's no magic, child. 120 are two minutes." That's how my mother taught me.

The egg was once again perfect. I cut a piece of polenta and put a small piece inside the egg. The yolk came out. I licked the shell as I didn't want it to go to waste. It was the best part. My father looked at me in disgust. He didn't like that. He didn't like many things. Eating for him was a necessity. "We need to eat for survival." For me it's a pleasure of life, and I was grateful.

Five minutes later, my father stood up and said he has finished and will go back to work.

"You always do that Papa! We need to rest a little. We are not slaves; you make me feel like one. Please. Look, everybody is having a siesta, some even sleep for a while."

"Don't be silly, it's Saturday. We need to be back

before twilight. Your mother is waiting for you to help her with the washing and cooking."

"But where are the others? Why nobody else came with us? My sisters could help mum with the washing. I am never sure what's going on in this family."

"They need to study and finish the work on our crop," my father replied. "Hurry up, John will soon be here."

"We've almost finished, haven't we? We might have to wait for him. I told you we'll finish on time."

"We still have a lot to do. I am going, you rest if you want."

I would have liked to lay down on the rug for a while, but I couldn't stand watching my father working, or anyone else for that matter. It's one of my many weaknesses. Besides, it wasn't so comfortable to lay on clods of earth. I gathered the remained food, which was quite a lot, and put it back in the bag carefully. 'The pigs will love the polenta, and we could cook the cheese the way mother taught me. I cannot wait to go back home and do it, I love cooking!' I thought with excitement, then I stood up, folded the rug and put the bag on the soil, covering it with our jumpers. The water was finished, and I realised we didn't go to bring a fresh one.

"Papa, we forgot the water. Do you want me to go and bring some?"

"Are you thirsty?" he asked. "'Cause if you aren't, there is no point, it will get warm in a few minutes. I'll go when we need it."

'It makes sense,' I thought and started working in silence.

One hour later we heard someone calling my father's name. "Giuseppeee. I am here. I hope you've finished as I am in a terrible hurry."

I raised my head and saw Uncle John waving at us. 'Omg, he's early and we haven't finished!' But as soon as I thought that, I noticed that there were just a few beetroots left. 'Thank God!'

My father took the bag from the ground and asked me to finish while he went to help my uncle to put the beetroots inside the cart. "Hurry up and when you've finished, come to give us a hand."

I didn't reply just focused on the job. A few minutes later, the crop was completely empty. No beetroots were left in the soil. 'Hurray!' I exulted in my mind and started running towards my father and uncle. I reached them breathing heavily. "You see, Papa, we've finished. I told you we will, but you didn't want to believe it. You are no man of faith."

Both ignored my presence, so I moved my attention towards the beautiful horse who was eating some hay my uncle gave to him. That horse was huge, and I was terrified. I've always been fearful of big animals, cows, horses, bulls, pigs. Sometimes I was afraid of the roosters too, for good reasons though! They were very aggressive! Fifteen minutes later, all beetroots were gone. The cart waggon was almost full and Uncle John tide up the beautiful brown horse to it. I grabbed all the things we had and thrown them on top of the beetroots. My uncle commanded the horse to start going. The beetroots weight a lot and were thousands of them in that cart. The horse had to gather all his forces to make the cart moving.

The roads in the fields were heavily trafficked, several carts were passing by in both directions. Some were full of corn, beetroots, or potatoes; others were empty coming from the village, ready to be filled with different harvests. My heart was heavy and I thought of how much I disliked that season. I couldn't stand the way the animals were treated. We didn't have a horse or a cow because my father wasn't home to take care of them and us, children, were not very fond of animal exploitation in general.

There weren't many trucks or cars back then, horses or cows were used to bring home the entire production, and not only. We walked behind the cart for one kilometre or so, until the road became more secure. My uncle jumped on the cart, my father followed asking me to do the same.

"I'll walk, Papa."

"You cannot walk for ten kilometres again. It will take you more than 2 hours. It's getting dark, we need to take the beetroot to the collective and be home before 5 PM."

"No, I won't do it. I can't. The cart is too heavy. That poor horse will die."

"Don't be silly," intervened Uncle John, "it's nothing for him. You aren't fat, jump on already, or I'll leave you here in the middle of nowhere alone."

I didn't like to be left alone in the dark, ten kilometres away from the village on a Saturday evening. I had no choice than to get on top of the beetroots, in the cart. I kept my breath, opened my arms, and grabbed on the two sides of the cart to be able to hold my body suspended. In my child mind, I thought and hoped that my body weight will have no impact on the horse. The beautiful animal didn't seem to notice, and it started galloping with ease. We reached the outskirts of the village in less than ten or fifteen minutes. From there we had other three kilometres till home. The cart slowed down, and I jumped off it fast.

"Cristinuza don't ever do that again. You could have hurt yourself. Next time wait for the horse to stop first. Besides, you should have stayed on."

"No, I will never, ever jump on a cart again. I thought I'll die. You have no idea how difficult that was. I held my breath for almost the whole way here. You didn't notice as you were speaking with Uncle John. Look at the cart, compare the weight of it with the weight of the horse. Does that seem fair to you? The cart is at least five times heavier than the animal! I cannot believe he could drag it all the way here. And with us on it!"

"Silly child, you are like a feather! It makes no difference for an animal! How will you survive in here?" Said my father with a sigh.

"Leave me alone, I am upset with both of you insensitive people."

We were at the *Collective* (the name gave to the association that took by force all the land from people) silos and left half of the cart to them—for the state. The other half was our part. That was the agreement. At first, we were supposed to take all these beetroots home because we've already given all the harvest from different pieces of land we finished two weeks before. But when the bosses realised they were not reaching the amount of the production required by the state decided to ask for more from those who had more land, and we needed to obey. To be honest, I was happy that the horse didn't have to carry all those beetroots into the village.

We left the *Collective* surroundings to go home. My father and uncle jumped into the cart, I refused categorically and started running behind it. I didn't like running, but it was the sacrifice I chose to make for the horse. At some point, the cart slowed down. I looked in front of me to understand why. There was a big hill a few metres ahead. I put a hand on my heart as to contain the pain that suddenly overwhelmed it. I rushed to reach my uncle who jumped off the cart too and was close to the horse. I knew what was coming. I witnessed this scene several times before. The animal was about to feel pain. I couldn't allow it this time.

As soon as my uncle raised his hand to hit the animal with a whip, I shouted, "Please, don't beat him, it hurts. I beg you."

Uncle John looked at me in disbelief, "What the..." and yelled to my father with rage, "Giuseppe, take your daughter from my sight immediately, or I swear to God I'll use this whip on her."

My father didn't expect that and wasn't prepared, but grabbed my hand to pull me aside. He never hit me and got very upset with my uncle for threatening me. "Don't you dare to hurt this soul! She's just a child, she doesn't know what life is yet. Don't mind her."

"What were you thinking? You know how Uncle John is, he could have hurt you!"

While my father was lecturing me, I heard the sound of the whip hitting the poor animal who made a terrible jump upfront from pain. I closed my eyes for a second to hold back my tears. I felt the power of the strike on my back, and I shouted as loud as I could, "Stop, please, STOOOP, you are hurting him."

My father grabbed my hand again and forced me to walk with him on the other side of the cart, away from my uncle who was saying to my father in disgust, "You have a very weird child, Giuseppe, not that the others were different. I have never seen anything like that. I pity you."

My father ignored him and tried to reason with me, "Cristinuza, this is madness. He's just an animal. They don't have souls."

I was sobbing in despair, "Who told you they don't have souls? But what does it matter? He's made of flesh and bones just like us! When someone hits you, you feel pain. It's the same for them. It hurts, Papa, it hurts. The body suffers, not the soul. You know that."

I was pushing the cart with all the forces I had, my father came close to me and start doing the same. "Cristinuza, he's just an animal. He was born for this."

"No, he was not! We don't have to hurt him! He's got a heart, you know. And it hurts when we hit him like it hurts when we get wounded. Why don't you understand this? Look at him, he's exhausted!"

"But how are we supposed to bring the harvest home then? We need to eat in order to survive."

"In that case, I won't eat anymore. I don't want to survive in a world like this. I don't like Autumns mostly because of this. We exploit animals, we hit them and they have no guilt. They haven't done anything wrong. Why are humans so merciless!" Thousands of tears were falling down my red cheeks. I was inconsolable.

"You'll see when you'll get older, you'll understand then. It's how things go. We have to adapt. Besides, we work as hard as he does."

"Maybe, but nobody hits us."

"Not nowadays... but it was like that for humans too."

I looked at my father, of course he was right. I knew he was, but I was suffering for and with the poor animal who was breathing heavily. You could see how hard he tried. My father was sweating, I was sweating and... next to me it was Uncle John all red and tired. He

58

was pushing too. The hill was over, we've stopped for a few minutes to gather our breaths, then we've started moving again.

I ran behind the cart, it wasn't long until home. We got there when it was already dark. The lights were on... Not the bulbs, the candles. The communists cut the electricity, of course. As every day for years now. I ran to search for my mother; she was weaving. "Mum, how are you feeling? Are you better now?"

"Yes. Where is your father?"

"He's outside, he's emptying the cart. They send me away, are upset with me."

"Why? What have you done?"

"Nothing..." I didn't want to say anything to her as she'd tell me exactly what my father explained before. They knew better, of course.

I went outside. Uncle John was gone, and my father went to check on the crop behind the house. I knelt on the ground, several tears were flowing down my red cheeks. I turned to God, "He will finally eat and rest now. Poor animal! Why did you do that? Why beings have to suffer?! I don't understand. It's above my capacities... You're mean, very mean. You make me cry. I don't like you anymore."

Suddenly, the outside light bulb illuminated. 'The electricity is back! Thank God. We could watch Jack Cousteau and the wonders of the sea life this evening. We all need some sort of entertainment.'

Then I went into the kitchen outside to look for hot water. I needed a bath. The door was closed, and it was very warm inside. In the stove were some shy flickering logs. I stopped and looked at the dancing shadows of the flames on the walls. I couldn't take my eyes off, it was mesmerising. I just loved the atmosphere in it. I didn't feel cold anymore. On the black metal hob was a huge silver cauldron full of hot water. The thick steam coming out of it was very reassuring. I felt grateful. I really needed a bath. I moved my eyes around the room scarcely illuminated by a candle, there wasn't electricity inside it, to find the bathtub. I spotted it on the floor, big, clean and grey. That meant all my siblings, and my mother too had a bath before, then cleaned it and left there ready for us.

We didn't have a bathroom in the house, we didn't have running water so no proper bathtub. The warmest room, like this kitchen now, was used as the bathroom. The bathtub, made from some sort of grey metal, was bought by my parents years ago. We all loved to have baths as often as possible. It was very important for us. We paid loads of money on it, and it was the biggest I've seen in my life. Very heavy and difficult to manage.

I took the hot water from the cauldron and poured it into the big bathtub. It was too hot, so I had to add two buckets of cold water. I filled up the cauldron again so my father will be able to have a bath too. He was addictive to baths, even more than us.

I went in the house to bring a towel and clean clothes. It was night time, so the pyjamas were appropriate. My siblings were watching the TV.

I locked the door, covered the windows with thick white curtains to have some privacy, and immersed my whole body in the bathtub. There were no shower creams or gels back then, so no bubbles. We had hard soaps made by my mother. They didn't smell nice, but were cleaning our skin well. I stayed in it for ten minutes dreaming about a hot shower in a proper bathroom. One of my sweetest dreams back then. Suddenly, I heard someone knocking on the door.

"Cristinuza, how long is it going to take? Do you need some help emptying the bathtub? I am outside if you need me." It was my father.

"Give me five minutes, Papa, I'm almost done. No need to help me, I'll manage, just bring the buckets in front of the door, please."

My father walked away. I came out of the bathtub, patched my body dry and dressed as quickly as possible. I didn't want my father to wait, it was late and he loved the documentary with Cousteau. He was his hero.

I went outside to find the buckets and using a big iron mug I emptied the bathtub and cleaned it for my father. I was about to go on the street to throw the water when my father came in and took both buckets from my hands telling me as usual, "It is chilly outside, you'll get a cold because your hair is still wet. You go in the house with the others and cover yourself with a blanket."

"But Papa..." I tried to argue.

"No but, do as I say."

I allowed my father to take the buckets on the street and I went inside the house, where my other family was watching TV. The light wasn't on, just the TV. Nobody moved when I got in, they didn't even notice.

My mother was alone in the back room, weaving. I went to ask how things were going.

"How long until you finish this rug, Mum?"

"I finished the rug last week, but I need to do one metre on the new one, so I could take it off. Your father is going tomorrow morning to sell it in the market."

"Do you need some help? Do you have enough wool?"

"Yes, go and sit with your siblings. I'll join you in a

minute. Has your father had a bath yet?"

"He's in now," I replied and left to watch some TV in the other room.

My father joined us twenty-five minutes later. My mother came a little later. I could hear her cutting the rug and sewing the margins.

Around 10:30 PM, we switched off the television as the programmes were over. Yawning, we all took turns to the toilet outside. Then we went to sleep in different rooms, but at least two of us were sharing the same bed. I was sleeping with my mother in that period, that's because I was the second youngest. My little brother was sleeping with my father.

That evening, as every evening for eleven years, I prayed for that poor horse and for every being in the Universe, hoping nobody would suffer the next day. I heard my parents praying too. But I couldn't tell for what. I realised I didn't eat that evening, neither my father. We both forgot. And the food was on the table. 'What a waste. Other people would give anything to have that food.' I thought with sorrow and fell asleep with tears on my cheeks and prayers on my lips.

I remember this story as it was yesterday, every time I see a dead copper leaf on the street. Autumns make me feel melancholic, and I wish for this season to never come. It is too gloomy. All the emotions experienced that day overwhelm me over and over again. I shed countless tears, ask for forgiveness and pray for that horse again, but not only. He is long gone now, same as my uncle. My father doesn't remember. He doesn't remember much from the previous day... If you'd ask my siblings, they will say nothing. It was a regular Autumn day for them. I was different. Everything was very intense for me since I was born. I lived with passion moments of happiness and sadness, and I remember a lot—too much—from my communist childhood.

I remember observing my siblings when they were doing and saying things. Trying to understand what they like and why.

I remember crying with my mother when she was extremely upset. I wished so much to take her pain away.

I still have a great recollection of the mud, the cold wind and how much I wanted to have a hot shower every day.

I recall the start of every scholastic year during the communists when they used to send village students in the fields instead of making them study Maths or read as the children from cities. All the discriminations, duties, rules, and exploitations; the shortage of fruits, toys, sweets and almost every vital aliment, the indigence... none of these will ever leave my memory.

But mostly, I remember how I felt when reading *Les Miserables*.

Father Frost and oranges

Christmas wasn't celebrated officially in my country during the communist regime.

Why? Because Christmas is about religion and God, and our ex-President didn't like competition.

Some say that Ceausescu was an atheist. It would make sense because he never spoke about God, went to a church, or was seen with a priest. No religion was ever mentioned in media (television, radio, or written paper). Our ex-president was famous for having razed to the ground several churches in the capital, but not only. So, yes, he could have been an atheist or a fervid fighter against God. I don't know.

If there was no Christmas, then there was no Santa Claus either, we would think. However, there was a Santa coming into town but was called differently. Not because my mother tongue is not English, but because it had a different name in my language too. I wouldn't know how to translate it exactly, but it is close to *Father Frost*. He came to visit children in schools and kindergartens, dressed as Santa Claus, but his name in public was *Father Frost*. At home, we called him with the real name.

Curious how I have never asked about this inconsistency. Again, I thought it was normal everywhere.

In schools, he brought us notebooks, pens and crayons and a candy maybe. All in a plastic bag, no fancy gift papers, and we were in ecstasy anyway, at least I was. I used to run home and show my mother the bag. I remember how I always took the candy from it, hid it in my little fist and fearful handing it to her while she was weaving.

"What are you having there?" she would always ask.

"Take it and, you'll find out. It's from Father Frost."

She would then stop weaving for a second, open one of her hands to allow me to drop whatever I had in my tiny fist. "A candy? How many did you have in the bag?"

"Just one," I would answer smiling.

"Then why are you giving it to me? Here, have it back. It's yours."

"No, I saved it for you. I don't like candies much."

It was true. I was never fond of candies, although some were absolutely delicious in that period. They don't make anything like that nowadays.

Why would a candy mean so much to me so I would write about it?

Because candies, sweets in general, were not vital for surviving so they were extremely difficult to find. Like toys, clothes, shoes, fruits, and everything you can think of. I said this before.

Our country was going through an extreme period of indigence, and not because it was poor, but because the President decided to impose all sorts of shortages to pay the debts he made without thinking. Therefore, electricity was given for a few hours a day, mostly very early in the morning, so the women were forced to wake up at 4 AM to bake bread.

The same happened with the running water. Timetables. We were not affected by that because we had no plumbing in the house. Only people living in the cities in communist blocks would pay that price.

Chocolate, exotic fruits, cookies, or sweets were sold underhand to friends and family. Same as meat, sausages, salami, any type of food made from meat was a real treat for many. You know this already.

Toys were even more difficult to find and I didn't see many in my childhood. I had no idea they existed, to be honest, and I didn't miss them. The Regime considered these a frivolity, not vital for surviving. All you could find in shops was made in my country, and the quality was outstanding. Unfortunately, for the people born in villages was extremely rare to see any toy whatsoever in the local shops.

My mother's told me that she heard stories of people buying toys from our shop, but she never managed to put her hands on to any because she wasn't a friend of any retailer.

Yes, you had to be friends or family or bribe the retailer to have a toy or something that wasn't easy to find.

Corruption was absolutely normal back them. Anyone could have been bribed. Teachers to give better votes and higher or false prizes. Retailers to sell you underhand all sorts of things. Bartenders for a better glass of vodka. Team leaders to allow you to stay home. Doctors to give you a shot or a certificate. Drivers to let you get on the bus. Office workers for any document. Every single person who had power over something was open to a potential bribery. At any time, for any reason. Yes, that was how things were going in my country.

That's why I never got a better prize in school, although I was one of the best students. I used to come home every single day with A+. My parents were surprised to see I didn't get the crown, but they were rules-followers, "never question who's got more power than you." They felt inferior because they didn't have diplomas, but I can assure you that my parents were smarter than most people I knew back then. I cared about reading, not the crowns, but maybe I should have. Too late now.

I didn't want toys, either because I wasn't an ordinary child, or because I was happy doing things around my parents. I used to spend most of my time watching my mother weaving, cooking, or doing the laundry (by hand), and my dad fixing the bicycle. I was mesmerised and didn't have time for anything else. Nevertheless, I had a doll in my life, and the day I saw her decapitated, it was one of the scariest of my life.

***

I was about five, I think. It was a regular Friday evening. The house was scarcely illuminated by some candles strategically placed in glasses filled with corn flour.

Why?

Well, weren't candles like the ones you see nowadays. They were very thin and forty centimetres or even one metre long. It depended on the use you'd make and the money you were prepared to pay for it. Votive candles. They emanated a reasonable amount of light, but also a black smoke accompanied by a terrible smell. These candles were white, and I liked that, moreover, they were useful when the communist regime stopped the electricity at regular intervals or without notice. Happened every day for whole my childhood.

That Friday night, I was in the house with my little brother, God knows what I was doing when an older sister got in. I haven't seen her for a few weeks as she was studying at a boarding school most of the year. I went to hug her, then she went to speak with my parents and other siblings. They were discussing something, but I didn't pay attention. I was happy to see my sister after such a long time. Fifteen minutes later she came to me and asks me to look out of the door window, into the corridor. It was dark, as I said, but I could individuate a silhouette leaning against the wall. I turned around and asked what that was. She then said to look better or go and check in person. I was afraid, I didn't like dark much. I stayed inside the house looking out that small window for a few minutes until I realised that was a girl, a little taller than me, wearing a fabulous blue dress. I gained courage and went to see who was it, thinking it was one of my nieces. —Yes, I have nieces older than me as two of my elderly sister got married before I was born.—I opened the door and got face to face with this silhouette. It was a girl indeed, but it seemed not to move at all. I touched her hand a little, it was kinda cold. Very weird sensation. I looked carefully, and as I didn't recognise her, I turned over my sister to ask who was that again. The whole family was gathered around observing my every reaction.

"Cristina, it's a doll. Isn't she beautiful?" said my sister.

"A doll?! What does it mean?"

"A toy, you can play with it. It is yours only. You can comb her hair, look..." she explained while grabbing the doll in her arms. The body didn't move nor said anything and I realised with wonder that she was made of plastic.

"Omg," I shouted excited. "She is not a person? She looks like one. I love her hair!" I hold her tight in my arms for several minutes. But she was taller than me and it was an amusing scene to watch.

That was the very first time I saw a doll. I've seen others after that, but they didn't belong to me. My brunette doll was the biggest of them all, the most beautiful, she was just gorgeous.

I jumped around for hours and didn't want to go to sleep. I am not sure if my parents allowed me to bring her to bed with me, I have no recollection of me sleeping next to the doll. Ever. What I do remember is the Sunday in which my doll lost her head. Literally.

I was playing with some children, maybe neighbours, perhaps my nieces and nephews. I put the doll on a table, pretending she was ill and I was the doctor in charge of visiting her.

I turned around to take something, and the next thing I saw was the head of my doll rolling down the ground. All of a sudden, without anyone touching her. Her long black hair was all over her face. She looked hideous.

I screamed and cried in horror for hours. "My doll is dead, and I killed her! I am going to burn in hell forever."

My parents tried to explain to me that it wasn't me doing anything to her. "A doll cannot die and she could be easily fixed silly girl," said my father. My mother assured me that I was not going to burn in hell for that, maybe for other reasons, but definitely not for that. My siblings were laughing with tears, but when they realised I was really traumatised, they went to look for my older brother— who was a very resourceful young man—and told him the story. My older brother put her head back in a few minutes, but I refused to touch that toy again.

All my siblings were disappointed, but none could convince me that was normal and I shouldn't be scared. I asked them to give the fixed doll away because the view of her silhouette scared me to death. Therefore, the doll with blue eyes and long black hair was given to an older sister who had another one, same height just different outfit and haircut. Both were placed on a piece of antique furniture in my sister's house, but I have never asked to play or touch any of them again.

When I think of this story now, I recognise that the murmured discussion between my parents and my siblings was about the doll. They were debating if the doll should be given to me right away, or wait for Christmas. Because they were more excited than me, the grand majority won and let me have it right then. Santa Claus brought me something else that following Christmas.

I now know that my siblings were asked by my mother to buy toys for the youngest of us from the cities where they were studying.

That doll cost an awful amount of money, but no one remembers how much so I cannot tell.

After that unfortunate experience, my whole family decided I shouldn't have another doll again. They wrote a long letter to Santa, explaining the situation and asking him to bring me something else, anything, just not a doll. Believe it or not, Santa followed that unusual request. It wasn't that difficult in the end, there was a severe shortage of dolls in my country anyway.

As I already mentioned, Christmas was completely ignored publicly. At home, people knew that Jesus was born on the night of twenty-fourth of December and we all celebrated his birth in churches. We were free to do that because my village was very far away from the Capital, but after the fall of the communist regime, many people recounted that they were not allowed to go to churches. Believers in God were constrained to hide and gather in secret locations, usually houses that belonged to unsuspected people like leaders, teachers, doctors and so on. In there they had to keep their voices down, which meant that were no singing.

This reminded me of *Quo Vadis, A Narrative of the Time of Nero*, a historical novel about the Christianity and the tortures they were subjected to, written by Henryk Sienkiewicz.

Winter festivities was called the period from the 27th of December until the 2nd of January. And although schools would all close on the 22nd of December, Christmas was not officially included in this winter festivities.

Rigorously, on the 24th of December, families would decorate a fir tree with lights, shiny spheres, candies, and chocolate, but it was called *Winter tree*, not Christmas tree. This was kept inside. To the day, it's still in my country tradition to keep the Christmas tree inside the house, however, in the last years, people have started to adopt Western traditions like decorating any sort of tree they might have in front of the house.

The perfume of the evergreen tree was inebriating, especially if you had a stove or a fireplace with crackling fire in the house. It was the best period of the whole year. The snow, the preparations, the cooking, baking, gathering together in the same room.

I loved the snow immensely. The first snowing day of the year, if it happened during the night, which was very common, my mother would wake up earlier than usual and asked us to look out of the window. My little brother and I were so excited that we couldn't wait to get dressed to go outside, but we'll run out without shoes, in pyjamas and dance in the snow. Roll jump and get completely wet. Pure magic.

Christmas time was heaven on Earth for my family. We had everything we needed, parents, siblings, plenty of food, loads of home-baked cakes and cookies. The siblings who left, either because they got married or went to work in faraway cities, would come home and celebrate with us.

The temperatures were extremely low, sometimes got under 30 °C, so we would cover our bodies in several layers of warm clothing, made from wool mostly. We would all gather and sleep in two small rooms. That's because we couldn't afford to heat all the rooms we had and used during more amiable times of the year.

In these rooms were only three double beds. Clearly not enough for fifteen or twenty people. So we would put some heavy duvets, amazing work made by my mother, on the floor and the children would fight for those temporary beds. I absolutely loved sleeping on the floor under the Christmas tree. Unlike my father who always tried to persuade us, the little ones, to sleep in beds instead.

"Cristinuza, you could catch a cold, please, go and sleep with your mother, near your older sisters."

But I was very stubborn and never changed my decision of sleeping on the floor. It was the best thing that could happen to me in that period, after the snow.

The stoves would burn wood continuously and hearing or watching the crackling fire was utterly mesmerising. Every night I would fall asleep watching the shadows of the flames dancing on the walls. I was so happy that I was afraid my heart would explode from too much joy. I have never experienced a more perfect sensation than that.

The saddest part of this story is the fact that more than a half of the country didn't have the means to buy and decorate a tree—that was considered the richest people's right. Half of the population didn't have a lot of food to put on the table. For many, home-baked bread, cookies, and cakes were just impossible dreams.

My family wasn't rich, but we were farmers and worked every day of the year on the land or around the house. We raised countless animals and birds, so we had plenty of meat for the most part of the year. We prepared sausages, salami, and other delicatessen that many were only fantasising about. We grew several types of vegetables and trust me when I tell you that was demanding, extremely, but we loved it. We had no free days, except Sundays. We went to school as it was fundamental to our education and we never missed a day. We loved school very much. But we also enjoyed helping our parents with the farm. We've worked hard and that was why we always had plenty of food. We've never starved as you might have heard other people saying.

Anyway, let's get back to Christmas and Santa Claus or Father Frost.

It was magical for us for all the reasons enumerated in precedence, but also because at Christmas we always met Santa Claus in person. Every year I sat on his lap and told him a poem.

He didn't come when we were sleeping, put the gifts under the tree and eat the biscuits. No, he would shout "Ho, ho, ho," knock on the door and wait for us to say "come in," and when he got in, was a perfect fairy tale. Red and white costume, long hair, and white beard, carrying a big bag on his shoulders full of presents for all of us. Body curved, trembling hands covered in gloves.

The youngest would shake from fear and emotion. Santa always knew everything about each of us and sometimes we didn't behave, so it was both a happy moment, but also a terrifying one. So many mixed feelings and so many tears shed.

The first recollection of him it's from when I was two. He brought me a red telephone. Not just any telephone, but the one I told my mother about. An antique one. A toy, of course. When I opened the pack, I couldn't believe my eyes. I shouted and jumped on my feet like a happy goat and run to show it to my mother, who would always sit close to the stove when Santa was there.

"Mum, look, it's exactly what I wanted! Remember when I told you about it a few months back? How did he know?"

"Santa knows everything, baby girl," my mother said.

It might be difficult to believe that I could actually have such a vivid memory from a very young age, but it is true. The image of the phone, the one I dreamt about, had a remarkable impact on my whole existence. The physical presence of Santa in our house, the tree, and the whole family reunited made me feel emotions impossible to describe in words. It was pure paradise.

I drove my mother crazy with that telephone. I

played with it every day for countless hours. I made it rang continuously, forming random numbers and talking with imaginary people. My mother begged me to stop many times, but I never did. It got broken in a few months from too much use. My father tried to fix it, but I lost a piece of it and didn't ring anymore.

If you think that my mother managed to still a fundamental piece of it, you have to think twice and here is why.

It was around September, the following year when my mother asked me what I will make my sister write the letter to Santa.

"What do you want for Christmas, the baby girl?"

"I want a telephone. Exactly like the one I had last year. Red."

"Are you sure you don't want a dress or a pair of shoes maybe?" my mother tried to reason with me.

"No, I want the red telephone or nothing."

Santa brought me *The Telephone,* of course. I was in tears as I really didn't think he will bring me the same gift two years consecutively. I was utterly amazed and couldn't stay in my skin from happiness. My mother could have asked Santa to bring me something else but she didn't want to disappoint her youngest daughter.

As I said, Santa was old, trembling from all his muscles.

"Why does he have such a long white beard and hair, Mum? And why is he wearing a mask?!" I asked every year after Santa's left.

My mother would then sit on the bed, took my little brother and me close, and told us the story of Santa Claus, "Santa was born many, many years ago in a very faraway continent. He is extremely old and that's why he's got such long and white hair. As for the mask, one year his sleigh broke down just when he was about to leave his house to come and bring gifts to all children of the world. He didn't have time to fix it, it was very late already, so he decided to take an aeroplane. Unfortunately, when he was going back, the plane crashed and got on fire. He managed to survive, but all his body and especially his face is full of terrible scars. He is hideously disfigured and wears the mask to not scare the children."

We were horrified to hear the story and were listening in silence. It all made sense, of course.

"But why are his hands and voice always shaking and covered in gloves?" I would ask again.

"Because he is timeworn and weak and because his hands are full of burned cicatrices. They don't look nice. You know what your cousin's arm looks like because he got burned, right?"

We both nodded "Yes" in fear, and my mother continued, "That's why whole his body has to be covered. He is also always in pain."

"But if he is so old and his body so ugly, why doesn't he ask someone else to bring children gifts?"

"He was born for this. His life would have no purpose if he wasn't Santa Claus."

"Does he have someone to help him preparing all these presents?"

"Of course. He's got many small people working for him."

We were utterly fascinated, shocked by the story and felt extremely sorry for Santa. We admired his will to continue bringing joy to the children of the entire world, despite being so old and tired.

***

Another Christmas Eve, when I was four maybe, I was

playing with my little brother when we heard a knock on the door. We've stopped playing and looked around the house for our older siblings. They were nowhere to be found. We've looked one at another as to ask, "what should we do?" when my mother shouted from the other room,

"Go and check who's at the door, children. Didn't you hear someone knocking?"

We didn't even know she was in the other room. We thought we were left alone, but because we were so focused on playing, we didn't notice.

Although the clock showed 6 PM it was completely dark outside. The house was illuminated only by the Christmas tree lights. I was afraid, I didn't know who was at the door, but I was the oldest, so I gathered all my courage and went to look out the window. In front of the door was a man with long hair and white beard. I couldn't see the clothes he was wearing. I started shouting that outside was a very scary old man and I ran away from the door. My poor little brother hid under the bed terrified.

My mother then said, "Maybe it's Santa Claus!"

Of course we were very eager to see Santa Claus but didn't expect him to get to our house at that hour.

"So early!?" I asked surprised.

"Well, he has billions of children to visit tonight, he must have stopped here first. Go and open the door, don't keep him waiting too long as he might think there is no one home, so he will leave to the next house."

This discussion took only a few seconds and when I heard that he might leave, I jumped and ran to open the door wondering where the heck were my other siblings!

"Ho, ho, ho," said Santa with a very trembling

voice. "I almost left as I thought this house is deserted. Other children are waiting."

He called me by name, and that was madness. Then he told me that I was a good child and deserved a great present. "But I will only give it to you after you've recited the last poem you learned in kindergarten. You did learn one, right? I heard you drove your mother crazy with it."

Of course I learned one, but I couldn't get my head around about how could he possibly know all that about my other siblings and me. While I was reciting loud and clear, sitting on Santa's lap, my other siblings got in. I didn't stop, but it was very curious that behaviour.

I finished the poem, Santa gave me a big pack, then he asked my little brother for a poem, but he was too afraid to speak and Santa was very disappointed. He almost refused to give the present to my little brother in tears. In the end, he gave it to him and shared other small presents to all those in the house. Even my mother got one. She opened it to find some orange balls.

"What are these, Mum?" I curiously asked. "Balls? But you don't play with balls! You can give them to Sebi," (my little brother).

My mother burst into tears and I couldn't understand why.

"Forgive me," I said feeling extremely guilty for making my mother cry. "You don't have to give them to Sebi. You can keep them for you if you like. Sebi's got his present." I was crying too. I could never witness at someone crying without doing that myself.

But my mother took a ball and started peeling it. As soon as she peeled a small piece of that orange ball, the house filled with the most divine perfume I ever smelled. The ball looked naked without the orange skin. When my mother divided it into slices, loads of juice fell on the floor. One of my brothers brought a plate and asked my mother to do that operation above it so nothing would go to waste. When that was done, my mother took the first slice and gave it to my little brother. Then she took another one and gave it to me and so on. In five minutes every member of the family had a slice of orange in their hands.

"Eat it, it's a fruit called orange. Very delicious." She was right, it was more than delicious. The delicate slightly sour taste made me fall irremediably in love with that exotic fruit which looked like a perfect ball.

I've never seen an orange before, maybe only on television, but as it was the black and white era, I didn't know they were in fact orange! There were many things we didn't see or imagined during the communist regime. We only knew how to work the land, follow the rules without questioning, and praise the leaders of the country.

My mother was crying from emotion. She saw oranges before, but she never tasted one. She loved them! It was love at first sight for me. I am not sure my little brother felt the same.

My other siblings must have seen those fruits before, I never asked, but I am guessing they were the ones buying those oranges. Most certainly, one of my older sisters brought them from very far away for my mother. She was known for doing wonderful surprises.

Every time I peel an orange, that memory comes back exactly as that evening when I was overwhelmed by pain from seeing my mother crying, and by happiness when understanding why she reacted so.

Oranges were my mother's favourite fruits during the Communism, and we always did the impossible to bring some to her every time we could. But they were nowhere to be found during the year, only in the winter, when the winter festivities got closer. My siblings who were studying or working in distant cities would go every day to look for them. They used to stay in queues for several hours in extremely harsh temperatures to buy a few at once.

Because the scarcity of these magical fruits, the retailers would only sell one kilogramme to each person. As we were a large family, one kilogramme was never enough. My siblings tried to explain a few times why they needed more, but nobody listened.

"Either you are buying one kilogramme, or nothing," was always their reply.

Some other times they were just sold two oranges at once, so they will go and sit in line in a different shop and the next day again, dressed in a different way to not be recognised.

***

A regular day of October, I came home from kindergarten and went to my room to get changed from the communist uniform. My little brother remained to play with some friends in front of the house. On the bed, there was a very colourful wide box. 'What is this and why it's on my bed?' I wondered. I took it and opened it with care. Inside were several plastic figurines, soldiers exactly. I had a look at the box, but I couldn't read so I didn't understand a word. It was obvious though that it was a battle game. A strategic one and I fell in love with the idea of playing it. I rushed inside the house to search for my mother who was weaving in the other room.

"Mum, muuuuum. What's that box on my bed?"

My mother blanked and quietly said, "I don't know. Go ask your older siblings."

I ran and called out aloud the names of all my siblings I knew were home. I could barely breathe from excitement. I found them working in the garden.

"What's that box with the soldiers on my bed?"

My siblings looked one at another, and one spoke up, "It's a gift for a neighbour of ours." A name I knew was revealed. "Their parents came to us and asked if we could keep it safe, so the child won't find it before his birthday. You know how curious he is. He will find it, no matter where his parents would hide it in the house. Please, don't say anything to anyone."

"I love it! I wish Santa will bring me one just like that."

"But that's a boy's game!" one of my siblings said.

"I don't care."

What do you think Santa brought me that year?! The strategic game, of course! I couldn't stay in my skin from happiness and surprise.

"How did he know, Mum? How does he always know what I want? Is he God?"

"Very close, baby girl, very close."

***

But Santa didn't visit us every year. When I was seven, he didn't come. My little brother and I were broken-hearted. My older siblings were terribly sad for us. We refused to have dinner and were sitting around the table with the eyes inundated by tears. "Have we upset Santa that much?" I asked in a low voice.

"No, silly," replied one of our older sisters, "he might be too busy, or he lost track of time. The world is huge, you know. And you are not the only children in it. Maybe he will just leave something under the tree this year. As he does for all other children in the village."

"But we want to see him," I said unhappily.

My siblings tried to cheer us up, with little success. We were utterly devastated, and the atmosphere in the house wasn't festive at all. Both my parents were away that evening. Curious thing. One of my older sisters went out for a few minutes. She came back all feverish. "Look what I found! It must have been Santa leaving them outside the door," she said while handing us some gifts very well wrapped.

"But why didn't he come in and how come we didn't hear him?" asked my little brother not at all content having the gifts and no Santa.

Our brothers and sisters didn't have an answer for us. There were looking one at another completely lost. My sister then took Peter, a nine-year-old-brother of mine, by hand and both went out. Five minutes later she came back without my brother.

"I sent Peter to look for Santa. Maybe he's missed the house or God knows what happened."

We were swinging absent in our chairs when the door was slammed against the wall with power. Peter got in all agitated, carrying loads of candies in his arms. "Santa, Santa, I saw Santa! I swear! He's stopped his sleigh for a second and left these for you," shouted my brother while giving us the candies. "He said he's sorry for not being able to come in to say hello, but he's busiest than other years. He also said that he's left some other gifts for you before, and he hopes you like them."

As soon as we heard the word *Santa*, my little brother and I jumped to our feet feeling very emotional.

"Where was he? Maybe we could still see his sleigh. We've never seen it. What about the reindeer?" I asked excited.

Peter looked a little confused and my sister stepped in, "Yes, maybe we could watch him flying in the sky. Quick, let's all go outside! Where did you see him, Peter? Show us."

"In the street, in front of the house." Peter ran to point us the exact place.

All my siblings followed him. Sebi and I were trembling like leaves in the wind. We had no shoes on and were wearing pyjamas, but that wasn't the reason we were shaking, we were electrified by emotion. The noise the snow made when my siblings stepped on it, is unforgettable. We all looked carefully on the ground. It was very dark, but we could actually see some traces on the snow. "Here," I said to my little brother. "Look, Sebi, he's lost some candies." I bent to grab a few. "So it is true, he's been here indeed. He didn't forget us, Sebi, he didn't!!!"

We both checked the sky meticulously, but we couldn't catch a glimpse of his sleigh anywhere. Peter pointed to a very faraway light and said, "I think he is leaving the country now. Can you see that light looking like a star? It's him, I am sure of it."

My sister took my little brother in her arms and guided his eyes in the same direction, "Do you see that Sebi? It means Santa was here for real."

Our moods changed completely. The smile came back on all our eyes and faces. We stand there contemplating the street, it was deserted. Some houses had the Christmas tree lights on, others were completely submersed in the dark. But I will never forget how peaceful and serene everything looked. We gazed inside our house through the window, and it appeared magical as always, but we didn't notice it before because we were focused on Santa.

We went inside, leant against the stove to dry our clothes and we talked about Santa for a few hours. Everybody had a story about him. We laughed, giggled and ate oranges. My parents were still not back. I wondered if my mother will cry again at the view of the oranges.

We went to sleep feeling blessed and woke up with the smell of delicious food prepared by my mother. The house was warm and peaceful. We had no carols to listen to. There was no programme on television. I didn't make a sound and watched my mother moving quietly around the house. I used to do that very often when nobody looked. I watched my siblings and my father too. It was my secret. I loved observing people and animals trying to understand why we do what we do, what makes us happy or unhappy, what we like and dislike. The differences puzzled and fascinated me.

My mother caught me staring at her, she came close and said in a very low voice, "Look outside. It has been snowing for hours. There is another metre of snow on the streets. Your father makes channels in the courtyard so you could go and play with your brother later."

"Mum, where were you last night?"

"Shh... your siblings are still asleep and you should too. It's holiday."

On the table were some oranges and the peel of one was put in a bottle of water. My mother thought of surprising us and make us try some water with orange taste. I felt immensely blessed, and I prayed for those who had no mother to cook for them, no siblings to go and look for Santa, no father to clean the snow, no Christmas tree and no special dishes or cookies on that day.

***

When I was eight, Santa brought me a fabulous blue dress with many frills. I loved it very much and spend hours admiring it.

I sat on his lap no more, but I recited a long poem that one of my sister's taught me—*The death of the deer* by Nicolae Labis (a great Romanian poet who died in an accident at twenty-one—allegations involving *The Securitate* still travel around). I heard Santa snivel, but of course, we couldn't see his face. He caressed my hair and congratulated me for being of such great help to my mother. I couldn't believe he knew that too.

***

When I was nine and my little brother seven and a half, Santa didn't show up once again. All siblings went to look for him, but there was no trace of him anywhere. It was raining instead of snowing. They couldn't stay long outside as it was very cold. We waited for hours melancholically and finally went to bed very disappointed. My brother and I sobbed for hours. One of my sisters gave us oranges and bananas, but we didn't want anything. I didn't like bananas, and my little brother refused to even look at them. My parents went to visit some familiars. We went to bed utterly devastated.

It was one or two o'clock when we got woke up by our siblings shouting that Santa was there. We opened the eyes, but we couldn't see much. Our siblings kept saying it was Santa and he would like to say *hello*.

My little brother started crying. He didn't like to be awakened and yelled at in the middle of the night. He looked at Santa very carefully and his crying intensified, "He is not Santa, he is Peter!!! Cristina, he is Peter I am telling you."

I didn't want to believe and I argued, "Why would Peter wear Santa's clothes?"

"Because there is no Santa! My colleagues told me, but I saw Santa every year, and I thought they were lying because they never met Santa. He never went to their houses, but he always came to ours!"

"How can you say there is no Santa if last year he brought me a blue dress and oranges to mum?"

"It was our father! Santa is just a fairy tale."

"What?!"

The whole sky fell over my head. It seemed the end of the world. I was in such a shock! I looked at my siblings and at Santa who took the mask off defeated. It was true, Peter was dressed as Santa.

"How...?!" I murmured heartbroken.

My siblings avoided to look into my eyes. None had the courage to speak.

"Santa is one of us? A myth? That is why Papa was never present when Santa was here? Why didn't I ask myself this before? How did you manage to keep this secret for all these years? Does mum know? Of course she does. She once missed from home... that year when Santa..., Father didn't show up... She went to look for him, didn't she?! And you too Peter went to look for him. But nobody found him. Why, where was he?" I asked all these questions out loud. "Where was he that night? And where was he tonight?!?" Nobody spoke and I shouted, "Where is he now?"

"He went to give presents to other children in the village. He is the Santa to the whole place, not only to us," said one of my sisters in a very low voice.

"What? How could he go and do that for other children, but not for us?!"

"It's because you both are older now and those children are very young. You can wait longer than little children. Our parents and we planned this very well, but this evening is heavily raining, and he went on the other side of the village, you know how far away is that. It takes more than one hour to get here. He couldn't get back in time because he had many other very young children to visit. It got extremely late and nobody can walk on a night like this. The streets are skating rinks—very dangerous. We don't know anything about them and are worried sick. We pray that they are fine and maybe decided to sleep somewhere else."

I started to worry too. My little brother stopped sobbing and looked at me scared. He was afraid for my parents. I tried to look back with a very reassuring gaze, but he became more and more frightened. He loved my parents immensely.

"That night he didn't show up again, was because he slipped on the ice and hurt himself very badly. My mother went to look for him that night and this one too. They are still in the village. But we have no idea of where to look for them. We went to a few places, but they left and didn't manage to meet," explained with sadness one of my sisters.

We waited for a few hours but fell asleep eventually.

When we got up the Christmas day, my mother was cooking and my father was sleeping. We forgot about Santa Claus, the gifts, and the sleigh. We were grateful to see them both home. We were also sorry for my brother who did his best to keep the myth alive.

My eyes opened that year and my heart filled with the most profound love for all my family. I now know why my father was never present when Santa was in our house. Why were my older siblings and my mother always away before the arrival of Santa; I know who bought the gifts and from where; who helped my father to get ready. I know how difficult was to do all those things and not be discovered. If in the late years, my older siblings were the ones in charge to look for the perfect gifts for the youngest, before my time was only my mother the one who took care of that and she told me that she used to go twenty kilometres on foot to find these toys.

Why on foot? Because when it snowed a lot we were cut off the world. She's told me that the snow was so high that every step she took, made her sank into the snow, so she had to stop and helped the leg to come out with her hands. It was tough and many people would have never done it. My mother did.

If you're asking yourself why did they wait until the last minute, well, they had no other choice. The toys were sold in the city shops two weeks before Christmas, and most of the time were already sold before seeing the shelves. Relatives, friends, friends of friends paid large amounts of money for specific toys. People like my mother, who didn't know any shop assistant, had to go from one shop to another, and pray God to find some toys, any toys for that matter.

I could never express enough gratitude to all my siblings and parents who did everything in their power and much more to make us feel children of the world, not slaves of Ceausescu, at least at Christmas. Those years were the best of my life, despite the hard conditions of life. But I knew that couldn't stay like that forever.

The 25th of December 1989—The end

From 1967 to 1989, Ceausescu decided who had the right to live and who had to die; how many children a woman should have; who was entitled to study, and who was doomed to work the land. We were not free to travel outside the country, we were not allowed to speak our minds, to protest or complain. He had all the imaginable and unimaginable power over our lives.

He didn't care you were a child, and all you wanted was to play with toys, no. If you were a farmer's child, you were required to help your parents and your school to reach the country's targets.

He kept us in the dark about the rest of the world, censored movies and songs, cut the power and the hot water for nineteen hours a day, rationalised food like we were living a war. He treated his people as slaves and expected them to endure all this forever with a smile on the faces.

In 1977 miners from Targu Jiu went on strike because of inhumanly conditions of work. The leader of the country ordered his army to shoot them dead—all of them. But the army didn't listen, and some changes had to be made for those poor miners.

Because these atrocities were never reached the mass media, we don't know how many of them took place. We heard rumours about thousands of killings, but we knew nothing for certain.

Every single person in the country was on their knees. We had no idea that the rest of the world had a different style of life, but we knew something was not quite right. We were hopeless.

There is a belief going around humans who didn't experience anything of the above. We think that if people don't know about the existence of something, they will always be happy with what they have. I completely agree with that. I am the first one to sustain this theory. However, we all wanted something we never saw on a daily basis.

We didn't have a fridge, washing machine, running water in the house, books, chocolate and so on. None of the people I knew had these either, but we watched some movies from time to time, and seeing how easier their life was, made us desire the same.

I didn't miss the chocolate, for example, because I never really liked it that much. But every Saturday, the day in which we used to have a *serious* bath, I dreamed and craved for a shower. I used to imagine myself having at least two showers a day, and that was one of my sweetest dreams. I fantasised about going to school for whole my life and read the books I wanted at the light of an electric bulb.

My little brother loved ice cream, same as my mother and most of my siblings, and if you'd asked him what would he buy if he had the means, he would have told you, "A freezer so I could fill it with ice cream."

My mother always dreamed about a proper colour television with a remote control.

One of my sisters was mad about coffee, another one about caviar.

All the children I ever knew wanted chewing

gum—loads of colourful chewing stuff. If everywhere in the world chewing gum was one of the easiest things to find, I believe that in my country was prohibited back then. I am not sure, of course, but no shop ever sold this odd sweet. However, I have chewed it many times after my siblings went to school, 500 kilometres away. In these distant big cities, foreigners would bring and sell loads of illegal or impossible to find stuff like coffee, play cards, cigarettes, porn magazines and chewing gum. This last one was made in forms of cigarettes and put in colourful packs of twelve. These packs contained imagines of football or tennis-men players, gymnasts, athletes or singers. Some of them were Romanian, and we were absolutely crazy for both images and chewing gum.

Once, my uncle asked a group of children what would they want him to bring them the next time he visits. I was in that group, and all of us, absolutely all, replied in a choir, "chewing gum." My uncle was shocked and tried to persuade us to ask for other things like chocolate, clothes, or religious objects, but we were resolute, "Chewing gum, nothing else."

***

In December of 1989, several people from Timisoara protested against the arrest of a religious leader they cared for. Of course that was not shown on television or announced on the national radio station. We lived very far away from the Capital and Timisoara and didn't have any relatives in there to let us know about this. However, my father knew about an illegal radio station that transmitted from Germany—*Radio Free Europe*—which had an hour in Romanian, for Romanians. I don't recall if they broadcasted every evening, but I remember how terrified was my father that someone could find us listening to it. Therefore, one of us had to stay on guard outside the house for the whole broadcasting period. We couldn't tell anyone about it and trust no one. *The Securitate*—Romanian secret police—had infiltrated everywhere. Anyone could have been an agent: your wife, husband, child, brother, boss, friend, even or especially the priest.

Thousands of people were incarcerated and tortured every day based on allegations or rumours. The only person you could trust was God because he didn't speak.

The Timisoara event has been spread in the country by the *Radio Free Europe* and gave people a push to start a real protest in the Capital. People knew that Ceausescu was heartless, and their lives were at stake, but the austerity and the extreme conditions outrun the desire of being safe.

On the 21st of December 1989, when the leader who oppressed his country for over twenty-two years started to give one of his regular speeches in the *Palace Square*—now known as the *Revolution Square*—many people began booing and chanting, "Timisoara."

Ceausescu tried to control the crowd by raising his hands but after a few temporary tranquil moments, and when he said that the minimum wage will increase, people couldn't bear anymore. The square became a chaos, and the intensified booing scared the dictator who took cover into a building.

I saw those images hundreds of times, and I cannot get my head around of why he looked so shocked about it.

Of course he gave instructions to shoot all the

rioters, but once again the army refused to follow his orders. Soldiers were heard saying, "It could be my brother in there, I won't kill my family. I can't." The Securitate then executed on sight several of these soldiers, but that didn't stop the crowd. In a matter of minutes, the population of Bucharest and other big cities were on the streets chanting, "Down with Ceausescu, Down with the Communist Party."

Ceausescu wanted to run and hide, maybe outside the country, but he was not prepared for that eventuality. I guess he was convinced that the country loved him and an insurrection was never a possibility.

He was caught along with his wife and on the 25th of December—Christmas day—before a kangaroo court, both were accused of many things, but what I remember was genocide and illegal gathering of wealth. Of course they denied all the accusations and refused to answer any questions repeating over and over again that they would only answer in front of the *Big National Assembly*.

Nevertheless, they were found guilty and sentenced to death which took place on the same day.

The trial and shooting were broadcasted in the whole country, maybe the whole world, I really don't know. We switched the television on outside the regular hours of airing because of the revolution and because Ceausescu's lost power over everything. My family and I were gathered in the living room. Our hearts were filled with mixed emotions, the sense of liberation and the sorrow for those people.

During the whole broadcasting period, we cried and prayed for the souls of the people who enslaved us for over twenty-two years. Personally, I couldn't watch that show. It seemed unreal and not right.

That year we forgot about oranges, Santa Claus or Father Frost, gifts, and celebrations. For us, that Christmas didn't symbolise the birth of Jesus, but the death of two people who had nothing human inside them. But we suffered anyway. I couldn't imagine myself in the same situation, it was too painful. That night we went to bed with a new burden on our shoulders.

***

Nowadays if you'd go and ask Romanians over the age of thirty-five about Ceausescu's era, most of them would say that we should have never killed them. They will assert that it was so much better during that period. More than 70% of the Romanian population wants Ceausescu back.

But I have my memories, like many other people, and I can assure you that Christmas day in December of 1989, all Romanians would have pulled the trigger. With no exception.

I am amazed of how people forget things like slavery, genocide, austerity, censures.

We were treated worse than animals, and we want him back?

It is true that my country is not doing well, but we have Freedom. We can travel and look for new opportunities if we want to. It is not easy, but it's simple.

My passport states I am Romanian, the truth is I am a citizen of the World.

If Communism hadn't fallen that year, God only knows what would have happened. We couldn't take it anymore. They had cutlery in pure gold and children were working the land to pay the country's debts.

***

Christmas has never been the same since that year. I wish I could go back and watch my mother while eating oranges or cooking her famous sweet pies, but life goes on and we need to adapt.

These are only my memories. I haven't spoken or discussed any of it with my family before putting them into words. They might have different perspectives, maybe even contrasting memories, but I was different. I was born with a remarkable sense of awareness and discernment. I've always been a very observing human being, highly sensitive, empathetic and attentive. I don't think there are many things I forgot since I was a child in that Communism era.

Every single episode of extreme happiness or unhappiness is forever impressed in my heart and mind. I forgot stories from when I was seventeen, twenty or from last year because they didn't mean much to me. But I would never forget any childhood Christmas when my whole family, nine siblings, and my parents, gathered under the same roof and waited for Santa.

Curious is how I never ever doubted of the veridicality of Santa even though I was an extremely observant child. It is true when they say that you only see what you want to see.

***

I am alone in my rented flat, tears are flowing freely on my cheeks. I wish I could be with my parents and my family. But my siblings are living in different countries of the world, and it's not possible to meet during this time of year. We lost connection, but even so, I wouldn't want the Golden Epoch back. I want to be able to eat an orange or a piece of chocolate whenever I desire. I want to be free to travel, see the world, and get to know other cultures. I want to keep my freedom.

I could have given a party or accepted several invitations, but I do not feel like celebrating. The Communist period ended twenty-seven years ago, but I still haven't been able to step out of the curse of it. All I can think of is what door should I knock on to get an opportunity.

Maybe Santa's? People cannot understand how I can choose to spend Christmas alone. I don't know how to explain why. It's a choice as I am fighting to break the chain of countless misfortunes and discrimination. I am fighting for the right to a decent future.

They did everything in their power to make me feel like a slave again. I had no right of expressing my opinions, to use the verb *want*, to complain if something wasn't fair.

I thought I will never get out of it, but here I am today in a country that voted *Leave* (Europe), an employee of a good company who helped me grow and build some confidence and self-esteem.

I have been working for years to fix what living under a communist regime destroyed. I came a long way, but I am not where I want and deserve to be. However, I am on the right path, and I am grateful.

Merry Christmas everyone! Craciun Fericit! Buon Natale! Joyeux Noel! ¡Feliz Navidad

Excerpt from

Ten Years in Italy, Three Weeks a Human

Deviant Love

The priest's friend and I fell in love at first sight, and that night he promised that I would never be treated that way. I believed him.

He took me to his place where he lived with his mother. A month later, the priest and the man I loved planned our wedding. I wasn't invited to the discussion. I overheard a few things I disagreed with, but I didn't intrude, just accepted my faith.

In November of 2000, still a virgin, I turned twenty-five. There was no party or cake for me. I didn't mind, 14th of November has always been just a regular day for me.

My future mother-in-law used to lock me in my bedroom every evening and took the key with her to avoid a physical union before the marriage. I wasn't bothered.

One Saturday after lunch, my husband-to-be wanted to rest and took me with him to his bedroom. The door opened suddenly, and his mother came in. I was outraged she didn't care to knock, she was horrified I was in her son's bed. The lecture she gave me was ludicrous. Her son said nothing was going on between us and demanded peace. I thought she'd have a heart attack.

A week after that, the man I loved took me on a weekend holiday in the mountains. She called him twenty times in four hours, and every two hours after that. I thought it wasn't normal behaviour, but he said she loved him dearly and wasn't used having him away.

That night was my first time. I felt no pain and no pleasure either. I didn't even have a chance to think when he started to shout I wasn't as pure as I'd said. Confused and hurt I asked what was he talking about.

"You didn't bleed at all. God only knows how many men you have had inside you!"

Utterly shocked I didn't know what proof I could bring to demonstrate my innocence. Nobody in my family spoke about sex. It was a taboo subject back in my country. During the communist regime, all movies were censored, I had never seen two people kissing. And as a Catholic, I knew I had to preserve my chastity until the day my husband wanted me. I was twenty-five, but still a child, utterly ignorant in that art.

I cried for hours, and on my knees, I swore that I never, ever, had had anyone touching me before. He looked at me with profound disgust and believed nothing. We slept in separated beds that night. Upon careful reflection, I remembered reading a book about the first time—Lucrezia Borgia or something— and she bled a lot. I concluded that there must have been something wrong with my body and felt awful. I spoke to him, and with tears in my eyes, I explained my fears. I don't know if he believed me or not, but he hugged me, and we made peace. I was happy.

Two months later, while having dinner, my fiancé

and his mother were having an argument about some of my fellow compatriots. It wasn't something new, quite the contrary. Not liking their allegations I ventured my opinion, 'Romanians are human too, we have the same rights as you. Why shouldn't we be allowed to buy a car if we have the money?'

Both stopped and gave me the same look and treatment as the woman from which they saved me. "Nobody asked you anything, don't ever dare to interfere in our conversations. Just who do you think you are?" the man I was in love with asked with fury.

Despite thinking I deserved it, I went to bed crying and promising I would stay quiet from that day on.

One evening, while having a bath, I heard my future mother-in-law speaking with her son about me. The pipes from the office passed through the bathroom, and I could hear them as clearly as I was in the same room with them. The things she said nauseated me. Twenty minutes of cries and complaints about my behaviour of the day. I had no idea she hated me until that evening.

I wondered if I should say something or ignore the story. After a short debate inside my head, I chose the second variant and felt sorry for her son as I thought it must have been difficult for him to realise that his mother didn't approve of her future daughter-in-law. In a week, I heard them four times, every time I had a bath. I figured it was a regular event and avoided the bathroom after dinner again. *"What you don't know can't hurt you,"* right?

Three months later, I was in chains again. Working from sunrise to sunset, without a penny in my pocket and no right to speak, I plunged into the most profound state of misery. I knew I couldn't marry a slave owner, and serve a woman who was supposed to care for me but couldn't stand the sight of me.

On Christmas Eve, the priest came to visit and stayed for a few days. A bedroom was required, and I prepared one on the second floor. However, my future husband decided to lend his bedroom to him because was bigger and nicer. It was a beautiful gesture, a sign of high consideration and respect, and I approved of it.

That Christmas morning, I asked him which bedroom upstairs he slept in. He said, none.

"Where have you slept then? You didn't go to a hotel, did you?" I asked, surprised.

"Don't be stupid, I slept in my mother's room," he replied as it was the most natural thing in the whole world.

After a few moments of disbelief, and intense debate between my heart and brain, I asked with the calmest voice I could gather, "Are there two beds perhaps?"

"No. I always sleep with my mother when we have guests."

My face turned red from the shock, I couldn't stay silent, so I shouted with fury, "There are three bedrooms upstairs and another one on this floor, how could you choose to sleep in the same bed with your mother? My brother was five when he refused to do so. What is wrong with you people?"

"How dare you? How dare you?!" he hissed through his teeth with ire. "You're a peasant, and a guest in this country and house, you are not entitled to an opinion."

I shivered, lowered my head, and walked out of the house wandering for several hours without a destination. 'This can't be normal in any country around the globe. I am not the crazy one, they are. I can't marry a maniac and live with his crazy mother.' I thought.

One day I expressed my desire to look for a job and move away from them. He went wild, and I saw death with my own eyes, but I wasn't afraid – death was less frightening than a life with those monsters.

Eight months and I'd been a slave to the man who promised me eternal love and justice. I needed to buy some tampons, and a phone card to call home and inform everyone that the marriage was off. I went to the bank to withdraw €10. The bank account my future husband opened in my name was empty. I asked him why when he got home.

"You all come here expecting to find a panacea for all ills. Well, now you see that this is not a paradise," my ex-husband-to-be said.

"Meaning?"

"What have you done to deserve any money, except upsetting my mother in every possible way?" he replied with rage.

"I worked in the garden since I came here, helped your mother with everyday tasks. I took down walls, painted, decorated, and built a new kitchen. I organised and cleaned every inch of your three-level house that wasn't taken care of since the day you moved in, which was twenty years ago. I was your gardener, cleaning lady, builder, painter, and so much more," I replied incredulously.

He looked at me with despise, "You've done everything you wanted to do."

"I've done what was needed to be done."

"What about the bulbs, you haven't cleaned any of them!"

"What bulbs?" I asked confused.

"The light bulbs from the chandeliers."

"Is this a joke?" I shouted.

"No joke. You haven't cleaned any of the bulbs which means you only did whatever you liked to do. That's why your bank account is empty. Besides, I took you on holiday for your birthday. Have you forgotten, ungrateful woman?"

I didn't know what to say. The people were nuts.

I found a job in a restaurant where they gave me a room. He let me go saying, 'You didn't want to be a queen in this house, now you should be happy being a cleaner for all your life. People like you don't deserve more.'

I left thinking everything would be all right, forgetting I loved the brute. For eight months, I fell asleep praying for him to come after me and ask for forgiveness. And he came, but when he told me that he was thinking to take his mother to a care home, I knew I couldn't go back. The woman called and accused me of turning her son against her, she cursed and insulted me with words I knew far too well by then. I promised myself it was over and I moved on.

****

Buy the book from
https://www.amazon.com/Years-Italy-Three-Weeks-Human/dp/1521236798

About the Author

Cristina G. was born in Romania during one of the most oppressive communist regimes that ever existed.

She is the tenth child – the seventh daughter – of a family of twelve.

On the 25th of December of 1989, the leaders of her country were shot dead. Christmas, a joyful celebration, has gained a bloody façade for Romanians with a sensitive soul.

Aged eight she fell in love with reading and realised that only books made her feel free.

In 2000 Cristina G. immigrated to Italy where she learnt that people cursed by geography are considered of inferior birth. Ten years later, deprived of dignity and covered in deep wounds, she went back to her country only to find out that freedom without opportunities is just another kind of prison.

Encouraged by her brother, Sebastian, Cristina G. dedicated many years to blogging. Now she is the owner of two very popular blogs in Romanian and one in English.

In 2014, helped by a British friend, Cristina G. moved to the UK where her expectations were not great. Here, against all odds and despite the Brexit Referendum, Cristina G. has finally managed to fulfil a dream she never dared to dream before: becoming a registered author.

Cristina G. invests absolutely everything into this dream: time, money, energy, body and soul.

All her books narrate stories of love and survival. Many are either entirely real or based on reality. Discrimination, immigration, abuse, self-growth are her main topics.

With a unique, eclectic style that focuses on human behaviour, in two years Cristina G. has written and self-published a couple of memoirs, a collection of short stories, a self-help publication, and three novels.

The reviews are outstanding due to her terrific determination, honesty, and passion.

With an astonishing background, outstanding determination, and remarkable passion, Cristina G. is a perfect candidate to greatness.

Her motto is, "Breathe, Love, Write and Believe."

If you liked this book, why not review it on Amazon or Goodreads?

Other books by Cristina G.

In English

- Half my Age plus Seven – A Sinful Confession
- Half my Age plus Seven – Too Good to be True
- iLive
- God is Weary
- Oranges at Christmas in a Communist Country - 2nd Edition
- Ten Years in Italy, Thee Weeks a Human
- Humans Cursed by Geography in the Pursuit of Happiness
- Racism Without Racists – The Truth about Immigration
- childless: How to Cope with Endometriosis & Vulvodynia
- Author for Life or for a Living?
- It's Never Game Over – An Informal Self-Help publication
- SOS – Single or Scotch? - Coming Soon

In Romanian

- Retetele Bunicii Invatate de la Mama – Volumul I – Sarate
- Retetele Bunicii Invatate de la Mama – Volumul II – Dulci
- Retetele Bunicii Invatate de la Mama – Volumul III – Prepara Porcul de Ignat

- Retetele Bunicii Invatate de la Mama – Volumul IV
- Cele mai Populare Retete ale Bunicii Invatate de la Mama: Mancaruri Nostalgice
- 41 de Retete Dulci si Sarate de Sarbatori
- 41 de Retete Practice si Simple de Borsuri
- 41 de Retete Dulci si Sarate de Post
- 41 de Retete Fara Gluten
- 41 de Retete de Chiftele, Omlete, si Aperitive Reci
- 41 de Retete de Clatite, Checuri, Prajituri si Dulciuri Varie
- 25 de Retete Rapide din Cartofi – Bucate Vegane Fara Gluten pentru Incepatori
- 25 de Retete Rapide din Orez – Bucate Fara Gluten Pentru Incepători
- Epoca de Aur – Amintiri din Copilaria Comunista - Coming Soon
- Trucuri Naturale de Frumusete si Sanatate
- Imi Curg Mucii Deci Exist